S0-BZQ-984

PLATO'S
THEAETETUS

The Focus Philosophical Library

PLATO's THEAETETUS

Translated, with
Introduction and Notes

Joe Sachs
<small>St. John's College, Annapolis</small>

focus <small>an imprint of</small>
Hackett Publishing Company, Inc.
Indianapolis/Cambridge

Plato: Theaetetus
Copyright © 2004 Joe Sachs

Previously published by Focus Publishing/R. Pullins Company

Focus an imprint of
Hackett Publishing Company
www.hackettpublishing.com

P.O. Box 44937
Indianapolis, Indiana 46244-0937

Cover image: Wendy Braithwaite

ISBN 13: 978-1-58510-101-6

All rights are reserved.

Printed in the United States of America

17 16 15   6 7 8 9 10 11

CONTENTS

Introduction

Plato's *Theaetetus* is the first in a series of three dialogues depicting one long interrupted conversation spread out over two days. The dialogues from the second day are the *Sophist* and the *Statesman*, in which the discussion is launched by a question posed by Socrates, asking whether there are one, two, or three kinds of people corresponding to the names sophist, statesman, and philosopher. There is no dialogue called the *Philosopher*, nor any that formally asks what a philosopher is. This trilogy, therefore, seems to have one member too few and one too many. Some scholars have conjectured that a symmetrical pattern may have been intended to culminate in a fourth dialogue, producing a tetralogy along the lines of a Virginia Reel, changing conversational partners from Socrates and Theaetetus, to Theaetetus and the Eleatic Stranger, to the Eleatic Stranger and Young Socrates, to the notional pairing of Young Socrates and Socrates.[1] Other and more astute readers have noticed that a dialogue between partners with the same name might be no dialogue at all, but the silent thinking within one soul, especially since thinking and dialogue are contrasted in just that way by both Socrates (*Theaetetus*, 189E) and the Eleatic Stranger (*Sophist*, 263E). Hence, the *Philosopher* would not be an absent dialogue but the image of the silent presence of Socrates himself, thinking his own thoughts.

There is no doubt that this conclusion is true to the way Plato writes, always playful, always pointing to something on display that is never quite grasped by anyone with whom Socrates speaks. What Socrates is and does reveal more about the philosopher than could any attempt to define one. And there is another and deeper reason for the absence of a dialogue on the philosopher, given by Jacob

---

1 See F. M. Cornford, *Plato's Theory of Knowledge*, (Library of Liberal Arts edition, 1957), p. 168.

1

Klein in the book *Plato's Trilogy*.[2] The central thread of that study traces an analysis of motion, rest, and being that emerges from the center of the *Sophist*, but is never summed up by any of the speakers in the dialogues.[3] The evidence gathered by Klein points to a structure in which being is not a genus of which motion and rest are species, nor an aggregate of which the two of them are independent parts, but a whole in which each constituent is what it is only by its togetherness with the other. If the knowledge a sophist would need to distinguish true from false images were inseparable from the knowledge a statesman would need to rule over human lives, the twofold inquiry about the sophist and statesman might be the discovery of the philosopher from two aspects, and the philosopher might be discoverable in no other way.

Again, there is no doubt that this interpretation uncovers a genuine intention of Plato's, one that in no way excludes the previous reading. The philosopher's activity may ultimately be silent, yet still be inextricably entwined with image-making and with communities of other human beings. But there is still a third reason why no dialogue on the philosopher follows the *Sophist* and the *Statesman*: one has already taken place on the preceding day. The richest, most direct, and most extensive presentation of the philosophic activity in Plato's writings is the *Theaetetus*. The question that guides that dialogue is about knowledge, but the question that Socrates asks first is about young men who care about philosophy (143D). It is in the *Theaetetus* that Socrates makes the famous claim that philosophy begins in wonder (155C), and forms of the word wonder occur in the dialogue more than twenty times. Theaetetus is shown to be a young man already accomplished in mathematics, but Socrates appeals constantly not to what he may know but to his eagerness to know more. A dozen times, Theaetetus reveals both his eagerness and his susceptibility to wonder in the oath "by Zeus." A parable about the legendary first philosopher is recounted in this dialogue (174A), and it is the only dialogue in which the word philosophy is ever used in the plural (172C). The old man Theodorus, who had turned away from philosophy to mathematics early in life (165A), is enticed into giving his opinions throughout a long description of the philosopher's life (172C-177B), and he gets excited enough to become quite long-winded himself about the battles between certain

---

2   University of Chicago Press, 1977.

3   See especially pages 47, 48, 53, 56-57, 60-64, 177, and 200.

philosophic schools (179D-181B). And not only when Theodorus is speaking, but through the greater part of the discussion with Theaetetus, the rich array of pre-Socratic philosophers is before us.

In the *Sophist* and the *Statesman*, the philosopher withdraws into silence, while the pair of guises in which he might appear is discussed. In the Theaetetus, philosophy itself makes its appearance, but the examples of that appearance gathered in the preceding paragraph make it evident that there is something external or peripheral about what appears. The portrait of the philosophic life painted by Socrates for Theodorus is full of dubious claims, and Socrates tells Theodorus that it depicts "the one whom you call a philosopher." (175E) In that portrait, philosophic activity is referred to as "philosophies," and Thales, the philosopher named as an example, provides no more than an anecdote. Once Theodorus becomes eager and talkative, it is gossip about contemporary philosophic sects that interests him most. With Theodorus, Socrates seems to keep the conversation about philosophy at a level one might find in a common room or lunchroom, rather than in a classroom. With Theaetetus though, Socrates elicits, from an intelligent and eager learner, a genuine effort to think hard. But what comes from Theaetetus always seems to be in the anterooms of philosophy, where wonder is alive but philosophic thought is never quite reached. The vivid presence of the pre-Socratic philosophers in the conversation reflects the things Theaetetus has heard, the opinions that are in him in an unexamined state. While wonder is launching him forward toward philosophy, "philosophies" are holding him back.

Behind the *Sophist* and the *Statesman* as one pair stands a complex conception of philosophy, while in them there is a silent embodiment of the philosopher. In the *Theaetetus* we have before us the phenomena that surround philosophic activity, appearing on its temporal borderline, in connection with a pre-philosopher, Theaetetus, and a post-philosopher, Theodorus. The pairing of these two men in one dialogue reflects yet another pair of dialogues, in which Socrates gives very different descriptions of the philosophic life. In the *Republic* (474B-475E), he describes the philosopher as loving learning with an insatiable erotic desire, but in the *Phaedo* (64A) as devoting himself to nothing but the practice of dying and being dead. In whatever way one might understand those claims, as images they are as different as one could imagine. The fact that the conversation in the *Republic* goes on into and through the hours of the night, while that in the *Phaedo* begins at sunrise and ends at sunset, may suggest that neither characterization of philosophy is more than half true. If Theaetetus could preserve and articulate the things he sees in his eagerness and desire, or if Theodorus could be rejuvenated into engagement with what he does not understand, a portrait of philosophic activity might come to life, but nowhere in the *Theaetetus* does this happen. We are left to fill it in for ourselves in the negative space the pair of them mark out.

While the primary topic around which the *Theaetetus* revolves is philosophy, the explicit topic its characters address is the question "What is knowledge?" As in most of Plato's dialogues, the question pursued is given no answer in the conversation, but it by no means follows that the discussion of it is therefore inconclusive. The way in which the living presence of Theaetetus and Theodorus surrounds and marks out the domain of philosophic activity is a dramatic imitation of the way in which the two main answers to the question about knowledge that are given in the dialogue surround and mark out the boundaries within which knowledge must be.[4] Of those two answers, that knowledge is some sort of perception or that it is some sort of opinion, the first falls short of its aim, while the second overshoots it. Similarly to the way in which Theaetetus has the energy and attitude of a philosopher in an inchoate form, perception has a lively, eye-witness, at-work quality that would rise to the level of knowledge if it could hold fast to anything stable enough to be knowable (186B-E). And in the same way that Theodorus wants to be sure that others are wrong, but can't rouse himself to the effort of seeing or showing what is right, opinion is the residue that remains when the active viewing and assessing of evidence has ended (189D-190A). The dialogue does not tell us what knowledge is, but offers us the occasion, invitation, and all necessary means to get hold of it for ourselves.

But why should such an indirect approach to a desired goal be chosen in preference to a more straightforward one? This is a question that might be asked about any of Plato's dialogues, but the topic of this one is especially well suited to revealing what the author is up to. Socrates himself states the predicament in which anyone honestly seeking what knowledge is must find himself (196D-E). If the need for an inquiry presupposes a recognition of our lack of the

---

4   On the general question of how to approach the dramatic aspects of a Platonic dialogue, there is no better introduction than pages 3-10 of Jacob Klein's *A Commentary on Plato's Meno* (Univ. of North Carolina Press, 1965). Pages 27-31 of that book address an aspect of the *Theaetetus* other than the one presented here.

thing sought, knowledge is not now available to us, while the aim of this inquiry could be achieved only if and when knowledge were to become known to us. There is something circular in all inquiry, but especially so when the thing sought is the very means needed for its own discovery. The innocent question that guides this dialogue thus forces us to ask in turn what Socrates calls "the most terrifying question" (165B), whether one can know the very thing that one does not know. Theaetetus the mathematician cannot answer in the affirmative, but Theaetetus the hatchling philosopher is excited at the prospect of following Socrates into this frightening territory (197A). According to the legend about Thales, philosophy was born when the ground disappeared from under his feet (174A). The question about knowledge becomes a philosophic one only when we are willing to suspend anything we think we know.

Anything Socrates might articulate about what knowledge is would hand us an opinion, perhaps even one more in a collection of "philosophies," but it would deprive us of the opportunity to engage in philosophy and perhaps encounter knowledge through the effort to know. It is characteristic of a Platonic dialogue that it does not tell us things but provokes us to do something. The dialogues are more concerned to prompt the reader into a condition like that of Theaetetus, perceptive, wondering, and making an effort, with philosophic activity in prospect, than to record the residue of thinking already done by the author. The ever-youthful Socrates even manages to nag the intellectually exhausted Theodorus into an effort to know. As Socrates tells Theaetetus at one of the times the latter feels particularly helpless (200E-201A), nothing will show itself to one who stands still, but one who begins seeking may find what he is looking for right at his feet.

A Platonic dialogue is constructed to be an especially favorable place in which to go seeking answers, and an especially frustrating place in which to think one already has them. This is not a reflection of skepticism, nor is it a way of speaking in code to certain favored readers while screening out the rest. It is one of the most spectacularly successful ways ever attempted to deal with the seemingly impossible task of writing philosophically. The beginnings of fruitful lines of thought are strewn in abundance through the dialogues, but none of them goes anywhere unless it is picked up by some positive act on the part of the reader. The suggestions to be found in the dialogues are not prepackaged into a "philosophy" but available to be taken up into philosophy; there is therefore no such thing as a Platonist.

A brief example of what I am describing may be found near the end of this dialogue. At 204B Theaetetus offers the opinion that a whole is not merely the sum of its parts; by 205A, in response to difficulties pointed out by Socrates, he decides that a whole can be nothing but the sum of its parts. A reader might be inclined to see something plausible about each answer. The interchange appears to leave the question hopelessly unresolved, but it is surrounded by examples that might help the reader go back over the question and get farther along. Syllables,[5] the example that leads directly into the question, appear to sight as nothing but letters next to one another in order, but Theaetetus points out that some consonants have no sound at all apart from a vowel; the sounded syllable therefore seems worthy of attention as a whole that can't quite be added up out of its parts. A little later (206B) it is agreed in passing that music is made up of notes, but a little reflection would show that the same melody can be repeated with none of the same notes. And the passage includes the non-auditory examples of an army (204D) and a wagon (said at 207A to be a hundred pieces of wood). An explanation of these examples would be worth something, but an opportunity to explore them on one's own—especially if the dialogue has succeeded in making the question about wholes and parts the reader's own—is worth incalculably more. To have heard Socrates argue that the whole may be more than the sum of its parts would leave us with one more second-hand opinion in us. To have explored the question ourselves with Plato's help may leave us changed, with a new activity underway in us.

The dialogue as a whole is designed in the same general way as is the section about wholes and parts. Every answer explicitly given to the question about knowledge proves to be empty, and empty in a twofold way. Theaetetus's answers are generated by nothing alive in him, but are things he has heard, and those answers generate nothing themselves when examined. They are, as Socrates pronounces them (210B, cf. 151E), wind-eggs. But this very topic of what a human being has inside is all over the dialogue. Theaetetus is compared to a pregnant woman (first at 148E) who brings forth a whole parade of pre-Socratic "philosophies" out of himself; thinking is compared to an internal conversation (189E-190A); memory is compared to a

---

5   The Greek words for element and compound are just the ordinary words for letter and syllable. In this dialogue, the syllable becomes the primary example of a genuine whole, something that has an *eidos*, that is, a form or intelligible look.

blob of wax full of impressions (191C); and knowledge is compared to a pigeon coop enclosing things that have been learned (197D). All around these images, the language of the dialogue is filled with a certain cluster of words: the verb *dunasthai*, the adjective *dunatos*, and the noun *dunamis*. The introductory conversation that precedes the dialogue proper alerts us to be on the lookout for such words, since Eucleides and Terpsion are associated with a philosophic school (a "philosophy") that denies that there is any such thing as *dunamis*.

The word *dunamis* is generally translated as "potentiality." If this is understood as possibility, the denial of it would make no sense. In this translation it is almost always translated as "potency" to get closer to its sense of internal power. And in most translations the verb *dunasthai* is invisible, since it is virtually always reduced to "be able" or "be possible." Plato's Greek had an ordinary way to speak of being able to do something, with the idiom *hoios te einai*, and in this translation it and it alone is translated that way. In order to say that something is possible, Plato had available a similarly neutral verb, *estin* accented on the first syllable, and here it and it alone is translated that way. When this translation uses such expressions as "have the ability," "have the capacity," or "have it in one," the Greek is *echein* plus an infinitive, a stronger and sharper formulation. Throughout this translation, the loaded and resonant word *dunasthai* is always translated with words such as "have the power" or "be in one's power," and the same is true of its cognate adjective *dunatos* and of their negative forms.

On virtually every page,[6] the *Theaetetus* prompts the reader to approach the topic of knowledge by thinking about potency. Even the example Theaetetus gives of his mathematical work (147D-148B) concerns looking at a straight line as a potent thing, able to become a square (a connection that is lost in translations that use the modern technical language of "roots" and "surds"). And when Socrates constructs an account of perception on the hypothesis that everything is in flux (156A-157C), he begins by positing that motions themselves would have to be potent in two different ways. The idea of potency introduces motion into the static realm of geometry, but also makes possible whatever fleeting identity there could be in a

---

6   There is only one stretch of the dialogue of any length from which all words with the same root as *dunamis* are absent. It runs from 176E to 184B, that part of the discussion in which Theodorus becomes most active. One might conjecture about why this word-cluster disappears there, but the fact that it does so only there is an exception that proves that, as a rule, it pervades the dialogue.

world of flux. It may thus point to the conditions under which a world could be knowable, but also suggest the way in which there could be a knower. If knowledge is something achieved, something that replaces ignorance and avoids error, there must be a way of having it when one lacks it and a middle condition between its absence and its presence, and these are the twin logical impasses that Theaetetus can find no way around (188A). The very possibility of knowing requires us to conceive the world and ourselves as being so constituted as to permit such a relation.

Now the idea that learning is possible only if the one who is ignorant has knowledge hidden inside him is familiar from Plato's *Meno* (81A-86C) and *Phaedo* (72E-77A) in the myth of recollection. Commentators on the *Theaetetus* from the first or second century AD to the twentieth have declared that the image of Socrates as a midwife to the pregnant Theaetetus is "equivalent" to the idea of recollection.[7] But Jacob Klein has shown that the purpose of Socrates's midwifery is not to assist at the birth of insight but to clear out the burden of opinions "fathered" by others.[8] The *Theaetetus* does not replace the myth of recollection with a new metaphor, but de-mythologizes it, or at least points to a way it might be moved from the realm of myth to that of understanding. Knowledge that is ever to be gained must first be present in potency, and the whole of the *Theaetetus* has a trajectory that aims at discovering what that human potency is. In fact, Theaetetus does catch a glimpse of what it is, but so fleetingly that he fails to hold on to his most important insight, and hence fails to secure it as knowledge.

Before we turn to the content of Theaetetus's insight, this notion of holding on to something that may otherwise pass by us is worth considering more closely. There is a second cluster of words that works together with the language of potency to permeate the texture of this dialogue. I mentioned above that along with *dunasthai*, a second potent way to speak of having an ability or capacity is to use the verb *echein* with an infinitive. "Having it in one to do so-and-so" would capture one aspect of this expression, but miss another, the sense that becomes prominent when the Greek language uses *echein* with an adverb to mean holding on or keeping in a certain condition. This dialogue is full of this verb, used in both those ways and in others, as well as in a variety of compounds with prefixes such

---

7   See Cornford, in the work cited above, pages 27-28, 15.

8   In the book on the *Meno* cited above, pages 165-166.

as *an-*, *ap-*, *en-*, and *par-*. Its importance is emphasized by the fact that Socrates uses a noun from the same root that appears to have been a rare word before Plato's time: *hexis*. The more common and relatively colorless cognate noun for a state or condition was *schesis*, while *hexis* appears to have been primarily used in medical writings. It is in its medical sense that it is used first in this dialogue (153B), not for any indifferent condition of any random sort of body, but for the proper and healthy condition of a living human body, maintained by exercise. Socrates transfers this same idea to the soul, and thereby produces a first sketch of what knowledge must be.

By learning and studying, Socrates points out, the soul maintains itself in a condition of understanding, holding learnable things in its power (153B-C). He uses the noun *hexis* at two more places in the dialogue, once putting it into the mouth of Protagoras (167A), who even in arguing that nothing is true, false, or understood, acknowledges that there is such a thing as education, a change from a worse to a better condition of the soul. What Protagoras does is invert the Socratic claim that there is learning without teaching, placing the whole activity of education in the sophist who manipulates appearances. But why then is what is produced in the educated person properly called a *hexis*? This question lies behind the third occasion when Socrates brings up the word (197A-D), to distinguish it from a *ktêsis*, a mere passive possession. Opinions can be possessed, but knowledge must be a more active kind of having, some way of having something in one's power. If there is a *hexis* of the soul, there is a power of stopping the flux of appearance, of stabilizing one's relation to thinkable things, and if there is such a potency, one has the capacity to hold the things one thinks not just in those packages called opinions but also in a live having-and-holding. This intertwining of *dunamis* and *hexis* emerges through the *Theaetetus* as the fertile region in which the question about knowing could be explored.

But these connections do not emerge explicitly for Theaetetus. Though he comes close, he cannot stop the flow of his own thinking in any way other than by letting it fall back into opinion. The dramatic moment at which he glimpses and loses his deepest insight is precisely the turn in the conversation from the topic of perception to that of opinion. The transitional passage begins (in 184B) when Socrates turns the topic of perception to the question of the power with which one perceives, and he declares Theaetetus beautiful (185E) when the latter decides that even perception cannot be the work of the body but must be a power of the soul itself. Theaetetus reaches the peak of his new insight when he names this power with the word *analogizesthai*, literally a gathering up but equally a power of analogizing, grasping timeless relations rather than fleeting things, and Socrates marks the moment with the verb *echein* in the imperative: "Hold it" (186A-B). Socrates is inviting Theaetetus to perform the very act he has described, to hold steady the evidence he has gathered up and see that the power of knowing can reside only in such a gathering. But Theaetetus fails to rise to this moment when he re-names the power of the soul involved in it as having opinion (187A), and all that he has gathered up from the preceding conversation is let go. The discussion must make a new start from the other side of knowledge.

There is no doubt that the remainder of the dialogue, about a third of the whole and the second of its two main sections, lacks the dramatic tension of what precedes it. But that does not mean that it has any less liveliness or philosophic importance. The structure, or trajectory, of the dialogue as a whole has the shape of missing the mark, and we have seen exactly where Theaetetus finally sights the target and exactly where he misses it. The Greek word for missing the mark is *hamartia*,[9] and this is exactly what Socrates proposes that he and his two conversational partners do (146A): take their turns at saying what knowledge is, with a willingness to make asses of themselves by making mistakes. Socrates cheerfully takes that role on himself in the remainder of the dialogue (195C, 209D-210B). And the particular and central mistake that Theaetetus makes leads to an extensive examination of opinion, aimed precisely at discovering whether it can ever be the same as knowledge, and if not, why not. The possibility of philosophy, as Socrates understands it, depends on just this distinction between opinion and knowledge, the very distinction that Protagoras denies (166E-167A). It is not an overstatement to say that the deepest conviction Socrates holds is that opinion and knowledge are different in kind (see *Meno* 98B). A deep and rich investigation is saved for us when Theaetetus's shot at knowledge misses its mark.

And the investigation of opinion turns up an unexpected bonus when it generates one more follow-up question. Perhaps what is

---

9   Those who are familiar with Aristotle's *Poetics* will recognize this word. Its meaning has nothing to do with a flaw. In fact Aristotle understands the tragic reversal to arise out of the hero's goodness. Something similar is at work here with Theaetetus.

missing from a true opinion but present in a piece of knowledge is a *logos*, an account that articulates what is known in some way that makes it intelligible. So at least Theaetetus recalls having heard someone say, though he can give no account of what was meant (201C-D). It is up to Socrates to articulate the question of what it is to give a *logos*. What follows is a subdivision of the section dealing with opinion, since it seeks a way to save a place for opinion within knowledge, but it holds a promise as well of being a synthesis of the two main sections of the dialogue, since the articulation sought also purports to be what brings intelligibility to that which is otherwise unintelligible. But Socrates from the start calls this hoped-for solution a dream (201D, 208B). In this dialogue, that word recalls Theaetetus's earlier observation that dreams can mimic waking conversation step for step and still be fake. It may be that any articulation added to an opinion would at best mimic the steps involved in knowing.[10] Even if one who knows can always give an account of the thing known, it doesn't follow that everyone who can give such an account has knowledge. We have no assurance that Eucleides, who wrote down piece by piece the *logos* that mimics a live conversation, has any understanding of anything that is said, though he checked to be sure his opinion was correct (143A). But we have the power to make the dead *logos* live.

This last subsection of the *Theaetetus* thus brings out most clearly what the dialogue itself is and is not. It is a treasure house of *logoi*, of arguments that give accounts for and against various claims about knowledge. It is not philosophy. It is an image that mimics conversation that might arise out of, or on the way to, philosophic activity. At best it may be an origin of such activity in a reader, but no one could predict what in it might spark in any particular reader an elevation to the philosophic level. The richness and variety of attempts, errors, new beginnings, and false turns that the dialogue presents strengthen its power to find and cross the philosophic boundary for a wide audience of people willing to respond actively to its promptings. Such readers may cross over into a kind of thinking that has evidence but is not perception, that holds still and steady but is not opinion, and that is not the conclusion of arguments and accounts but the source of them.

---

10   Compare the claim at *Republic* 533B-C that mathematics dreams about what is, since it gives its accounts always under the sway of hypotheses, lacking any power to turn them into knowledge.

Acknowledgments

This translation, and any understanding of the *Theaetetus* that led to its making, came to be over the course of many years, through many readings, and with the help of many people. I am grateful especially to:

Robert Bart, with whom I first read the dialogue when I was an undergraduate.

Seth Benardete, in whose class at the Graduate Faculty of the New School in New York I began to discover and appreciate the wealth of its content.

A small group of colleagues at St. John's College who met, once a week throughout a year in the early 1980s, in what one might laughingly call their spare time, out of a genuine love of learning, to discuss the dialogue.

Stewart Umphrey, who gave an extraordinary lecture on it later in that decade.

A group of five wonderful students in an intensive class in the Fall of 2001, who led me into every corner of the text.

Seth Benardete once again, whose translation of the dialogue was the only one I found to be accurate and perceptive, though it is not easy to read.

Stewart Umphrey once again, who generously read the whole of a draft of this translation and made many suggestions that have improved it.

And last and most of all, Eric Salem, who read the draft translation with painstaking care and a wise judgment, and made hundreds of suggestions for improvement, which I have followed *hôs epi to polu*.

Annapolis, Maryland

Summer, 2003

PLATO'S THEAETETUS

Eucleides, Terpsion

Eu: Right now[1] in from the country, Terpsion, or a while   *142A*
ago?

Terp: A fairly good while ago. In fact I was looking for you
at the marketplace, and wondering that I couldn't find
you.

Eu: It's because I wasn't in town.

Terp: But where?

Eu: Going down to the harbor I happened on Theaetetus,
being carried to Athens from Corinth, from the army
camp.

Terp: Living or dead?

Eu: Living, but just barely. He's in a bad way from some   *B*
wounds, but even worse, the sickness that's come on
the army has taken him.

Terp: Not the dysentery?

Eu: Yes.

Terp: What a man you say is in danger!

Eu: A fine and good gentleman, Terpsion, seeing as how
even now I heard some people praising him highly in
connection with the battle.

---

1   The first word of a Platonic dialogue is often a playful reference to its central
concern. Of the two main contenders for the title of knowledge, perception has
a "right-now" aspect that opinion lacks.

Terp: And there's nothing out of place about that. It would have been much more to be wondered at if he hadn't

C   been that way. But how is it that he didn't break his journey here in Megara[2]?

Eu: He was hurrying home, for I kept begging and advising it, but he didn't want to. So I escorted him, and as I came back again I recollected Socrates and wondered at how prophetically he spoke, both about other things and particularly about this man. For it seems to me he happened upon him a little before his own death, when Theaetetus was a young man, and when he had been with him and conversed with him he greatly admired his nature. And when I went to Athens he recounted to me in detail the words spoken in his conversation with him—and well worth hearing they were—and he said it was utterly necessary that this man would come to be talked about if he should reach the prime of life.

Terp: He spoke the truth about that at least, it seems. But what were their words? Could you recount them?

Eu: No, by Zeus; at least they're not on the tip of my tongue

143A   that way. But I did write down notes at the time as soon as I got home, and later, as I recollected at leisure, I kept on writing, and as often as I got to Athens, asking Socrates again and again about what I didn't remember, I made corrections when I came back here, so that something pretty much like the whole talk is written down for me.

Terp: True. I heard about it from you before, and in fact I've been killing all this time here intending to tell you to show it. But what prevents us from going through it now? At any rate I also need to rest, since I came from the country.

B   **Eu:** But I myself also escorted Theaetetus as far as Erineum, so that I wouldn't be displeased at resting. Let's do so then, and the boy will read to us at the same time that we rest.

---

2   Aristotle, in Bk. IX, Chap. 3 of the Metaphysics, reports that Megara was identified with the philosophic claim that there are no potentialities before things happen.

Terp: You've said the correct thing.

Eu: Here's the book, Terpsion, and this is the way I wrote down the talk: not with Socrates recounting it to me as he recounted it, but with him speaking with those whom he said he spoke with. And he said he spoke with the geometer Theodorus and with Theaetetus. So in order that the narrations between the speeches *C* would not cause trouble in the writing—such as "and I said" or "and I replied" whenever Socrates spoke about himself, or "he concurred" or "he did not agree" about the person who answered—on account of these things I wrote it as though he was conversing with them, and took out things like that.

Terp: And there's nothing out of the way in that, Eucleides.

Eu: So, boy, take the book and read.

* * *

Socrates, Theodorus, Theaetetus

Soc: If I cared more about things in Cyrene, Theodorus, *D* I'd ask you about things there and about the people, whether there are any of the local young people who pay attention to geometry or to any other sort of philosophy. But as things are, I love them less than those who are here, and I'm more eager to know which of our young people are considered likely to make a decent showing. Now I myself look into these things to the limit of my power, and I question those others whom I see that the young people want to associate with. Not a few of them come around you, and with justice, for you are deserving of it both for *E* other reasons and on account of geometry. So if you've happened upon anyone worthy of mention, I would hear the news with pleasure.

Theo: Surely, Socrates, it is well worthwhile for me to tell and you to hear about a young man of this sort that I have happened upon among your fellow citizens.

And if he were good-looking, I would be afraid to say too much, lest I seem to someone to be in love with him. But as it is—and don't be annoyed at me—he is not good-looking but looks like you, both in the squashed-in-ness of his nose and the bulging out of his eyes, though he has these features less than you do. I'm speaking quite fearlessly. But know well that of those I have ever yet happened upon—and I have been around very many—I have never yet perceived anyone so wonderfully well off by nature. For someone who is quick at learning, in a way that is difficult for anyone else, to be also surpassingly gentle, and on top of these things manly beyond anyone whatever, I would not have supposed could happen, nor do I see it happen. Instead, those who are sharp and quick and remember the way he does also for the most part have quick swings of moods, and shooting off, they are carried around like boats without ballast; they are by nature more frenzied than manly, while those in turn who are more weighty are somehow sluggish in their approach to learning and are filled with forgetfulness. But he advances toward learning and inquiring so smoothly and unstumblingly and efficiently, with so much gentleness, like a stream of oil flowing without a sound, that one wonders at his accomplishing these things in this way while being of such an age.

144A

B

Soc: You bring good news. But which of our citizens does he come from?

C   **Theo:** I've heard the name, but I don't remember it. But he himself is one of these people right here coming toward us, the one in the middle. For just now in the outer course of the track he and these companions of his were rubbing themselves down, and now they seem to me to be oiled and coming here. Just see whether you recognize him.

Soc: I do recognize him: he is the son of Euphronius of Sunium, and in fact, my friend, he was exactly the sort of man you described this one to be, and well thought of in other respects, and certainly he also left a very large property. But I don't know the young man's name.

Theo: Theaetetus is his name, Socrates, though as to the property, it seems to me that some of the trustees wasted it away. But even so, as far as generosity with money is concerned, he is wonderful, Socrates. **D**

Soc: You describe a well-born man. Call him over here to sit next to me.

Theo: These things will be done. Over here, Theaetetus, by Socrates.

Soc: Exactly so, Theaetetus, in order that I too may look closely at myself and see what sort of face I have, since **E** Theodorus says I have one that's like you. But if each of the pair of us had a lyre, and he said they were tuned alike, should we trust him straight off, or consider whether he was speaking as one skilled in music?

Theae: We should consider it.

Soc: Then if we found out that he was of that sort, we should trust him, but if he were unmusical distrust him?

Theae: True.

Soc: But now, I suppose, if anything about the likeness of faces is of concern to us, we should consider whether **145A** he was speaking as one skilled at drawing or not.

Theae: It seems that way to me.

Soc: Well, is Theodorus skilled at painting portraits?

Theae: No, as far as I know at any rate.

Soc: And not skilled at geometry either?

Theae: It's completely beyond doubt that he is, Socrates.

Soc: And skilled at astronomy and calculation and music, and as many things as have a bearing on education?

Theae: As far as I'm concerned, he seems to be.

Soc: So if he says that we're alike in anything having to do with the body, whether praising or blaming us in any respect, it's not worth paying very much attention to him.

Theae: Maybe not.

B   **Soc:** But what if he were to praise the soul of one of us for virtue and wisdom? Isn't it worthwhile for the one who hears it to be eager to take a close look at the one who is praised, and for that one eagerly to display himself?

Theae: Very much so, Socrates.

Soc: Well then, dear Theaetetus, it's time for you to display and for me to inspect. Know well that, although Theodorus has praised many people to me, both foreigners and townspeople, he has praised no one yet the way he praised you just now.

Theae: That might well be, Socrates, but see whether he
C   wasn't being playful when he said it.

Soc: That's not Theodorus's way. But don't go back on the things we agreed to by claiming he spoke playfully, or he will also be forced to testify to it, for absolutely no one would impeach him. Just be brave and stick by the agreement.

Theae: Then I have to do these things, if it seems so to you.

Soc: Tell me, then: I presume you learn some things belonging to geometry from Theodorus?

Theae: I do.

D   **Soc:** And having to do with astronomy and harmony and calculation?

Theae: I'm certainly eager to.

Soc: I am too, my boy, from him and from others whom I suppose to understand any of these things. But in spite of the fact that I have some other things about these subjects down fairly well, I am still at a loss about a little something, which ought to be examined with you and with them. Tell me, isn't learning becoming wiser about that which one learns?

Theae: How could it be otherwise?

Soc: But it's certainly by wisdom, I suppose, that the wise are wise.

Theae: Yes.

Soc: And this thing certainly doesn't differ at all from   *E*
knowledge, does it?

Theae: What sort of thing?

Soc: Wisdom. Or aren't those very things people know also
things they are wise about?

Theae: What about it?

Soc: Knowledge and wisdom are therefore the same thing?

Theae: Yes.

Soc: Well it's this very thing that I'm at a loss about, and I
don't have the power to get it adequately by myself,
just exactly what knowledge is. So do we have it in us   *146A*
to state it? What do you folks say? Which of us should
speak first? And the one who makes a mistake, and
always whoever makes a mistake will sit down, an
ass, as children say when they play ball; but whoever
survives without making a mistake will be our king
and order us to answer whatever he wants. Why are
you folks silent? I hope I'm not being tactless in any
way, Theodorus, as a result of my love of talk, because
I'm eager to make us have a discussion and become
friends and conversant with each other?

Theo: Least of all, Socrates, would that sort of thing be   *B*
tactless, but tell one of the young men to answer
you. I'm unaccustomed to this sort of discussion, and
moreover I'm not of an age to get accustomed to it. But
it would be appropriate for these fellows, and would
benefit them much more; for youth holds in it the
capacity for improvement in everything for the one
who is young. Come on then, just as you started; don't
let go of Theaetetus, but question him.

Soc: So, Theaetetus, you hear what Theodorus says, who I   *C*
suppose is not someone you would wish to disobey, and
it isn't even legitimate for a younger person to disobey a
wise man in connection with such things when he gives
an order. Just speak up well and like a well bred man:
what does knowledge seem to you to be?

Theae: I have to then, Socrates, since in fact you both tell me to. For in any case, if I make any mistake, you will both correct me.

Soc: Very much so, at least if we are able to.

Theae: It seems to me, then, both that the things one might learn from Theodorus are pieces of knowledge, geometry and what you went over just now, and also skill at leather-cutting and the arts of the other craftsmen—each and every one of these is nothing other than knowledge.

D

Soc: It's certainly well bred and generous of you, dear fellow, when you're asked for one thing, to give many and varied things instead of something simple.

Theae: Whatever do you mean by that, Socrates?

Soc: Perhaps nothing, though I will tell you what I am thinking. When you speak of skill at leatherworking, you mean nothing other than knowledge of the workmanship of shoes?

Theae: Nothing else.

E

Soc: And what about when it's skill at carpentry? You mean nothing other than knowledge of the workmanship of wooden equipment?

Theae: Nothing else in this case either.

Soc: Then in both cases, you are marking out that which each sort of knowledge is about?

Theae: Yes.

Soc: But what was asked, Theaetetus, was not that, what things knowledge is about, or how many pieces of knowledge there are; for we didn't ask it because we wanted to count them, but in order to discern knowledge itself—whatever that is. Or is there nothing in what I'm saying?

Theae: What you're saying is entirely correct.

147A

Soc: Then also consider this: if someone were to ask us about any of the lowly things here at hand, for instance about mud, just what it is, if we were to answer him that it's the mud that's used by potters, and the mud used by furnace makers and by brick makers, wouldn't we be ridiculous?

Theae: Maybe.

Soc: Sure—first of all for supposing that, whenever we mention mud, the questioner would understand it from our answer, whether we tack on "used by doll makers" or used by any other craftsmen whatever. Or do you suppose that anyone understands any name of anything when he doesn't know what it is?

B

Theae: By no means.

Soc: Therefore, one who doesn't know knowledge won't understand the knowledge of shoes either.

Theae: No.

Soc: Therefore, whoever is ignorant of knowledge doesn't understand leatherworking skill or any other art either.

Theae: That's the way it is.

Soc: Therefore, the answer to the one who asks what knowledge is was ridiculous when it gave as an answer the name of any art. For it gives as an answer what knowledge is about when this is not what was asked.

C

Theae: It seems so.

Soc: In the next place, one who has it in him, surely, to answer in a low-key and brief way, is going around along an endless road. For example, in the question about mud, it would surely be a low-key and simple thing to say that mud would be earth mixed with liquid, and to say goodbye to whoever uses it.

Theae: It's easy, Socrates, now that it's made apparent this way. But there's a good chance you're asking for the sort of thing that also occurred to us ourselves just now when we were talking, to me and to this Socrates, who has the same name as you.

D

Soc: What sort of thing was that, Theaetetus?

Theae: Theodorus here was diagramming something for us about potencies,[3] demonstrating about the potential side of the three-foot square and about that of the five-foot square that they are not commensurable in length with the foot-long line, and demonstrating in this way as he picked out each of them one by one up to the potential side of the seventeen-foot square; at that one, for some reason, he got tangled up.[4] So something of this sort occurred to us: since the potential squares are obviously infinite in multitude, we would try to gather them together into some one thing, in which we could address our speech to all these potential squares.

E

Soc: And did you find anything of the sort?

Theae: It seems to me we did. But you take a look too.

Soc: Tell me.

Theae: We divided all number in two. Imaging the sort with the potency to come into being as an equal times an equal by the shape of a square, we called it by the names square and equilateral.

Soc: Well done indeed.

148A

Theae: Then for the sort that are between those, among which are three and five and every number without the potency to come into being as an equal times an equal, though it does come into being as a greater times a lesser or a lesser times a greater, and it's always a greater and a lesser side that contain it, imaging this sort in turn by the shape of the oblong, we called it oblong number.

Soc: Very beautiful. But what came after that?

---

3   This word is used by Euclid in his *Elements*, Book X, Definition 4 and Proposition 17. Book X is thought to contain the work of Theaetetus. The Greek word for the power of a line to generate a square is just the word for potentiality in general, all of which is denied by the Megarian philosophers.

4   The proofs Theodorus was giving are difficult, and a single pattern will not work for all cases. In a recent article in the *St. John's Review*, Vol. XLVI, No. 1 (2000), Amirthanayagam David shows how the two different patterns of proof needed for three and five work up to, but not for, the case of seventeen.

Theae: As many lines as generate squares for the equilateral plane numbers, we defined as lengths, but as many as generate the squares for the oblong numbers, we defined as potencies, since they are not commensurable with those others in length, but only in the areas which they have the potency to generate. And there's another thing of this sort about solids.

B

Soc: That's the best in human power, boys.[5] So it seems to me that Theodorus will not be tangled up in false testimony.

Theae: And yet, Socrates, I wouldn't have the power to answer what you ask about knowledge the same way as about length and potency, even though you seem to me to be looking for something of that sort. So Theodorus appears false back again.

Soc: What? If in praising you for running he said he had never yet happened upon any of the young people who was so skilled at running, and then while racing you were defeated by the fastest man at the peak of his powers, do you suppose it would have been any less true for this man here to praise you?

C

Theae: Not I.

Soc: But knowledge, as I was just now speaking of it, do you suppose that to be a small thing to find out and not something for those who are top-notch in every way?

Theae: By Zeus, not I; it's precisely something for top-notch people.

Soc: Then be confident about yourself and believe there's something in what Theodorus says, and show eagerness in every way, both about everything else and about knowledge, to get hold of a statement saying just exactly what it is.

D

---

5   What Theaetetus accomplished was not just an act of naming, but something that leads immediately to a general proof. It is given as the fourth part of Euclid's proposition X, 9, and requires only two steps, as compared with the great technical complexity involved in proving the same thing case by case. It seems likely that Socrates "saw" the proof implicit in Theaetetus's highly compact report.

Theae: As far as it depends on eagerness, Socrates, it will come to light.

Soc: Come on then—you led the way beautifully just now—try to imitate your answer about potential squares, and just as you encompassed them all, many as they are, in one look,[6] so too try to address the many sorts of knowledge in one statement.

E
Theae: But know well, Socrates, that I've tried my hand many times at examining this, hearing the questions that are carried off from you, but I don't have the power to persuade myself either that I say anything adequately or that I hear anyone else speaking in the way that you call for. But on the other hand, I don't have the power to get myself free from caring about it.

Soc: Dear Theaetetus, it's not because you're empty that you're laboring; you're in labor because you're pregnant.

Theae: I don't know about that, Socrates. I'm just telling you what I've experienced.

149A
Soc: So then, silly fellow, you haven't heard that I am the son of a thoroughly pure-bred and stern midwife, Phaenarete?

Theae: That I have heard before.

Soc: Then have you heard also that I practice the same art?

Theae: By no means.

Soc: Then know well that I do; but don't expose me to the others, my companion, for it has escaped detection that I have this art. Other people, since they don't know it, don't say that about me, but they say that I'm a most unsettling person and that I make people be at a loss.[7]

---

6   This is the first occurrence in this dialogue of the word *eidos*, a favorite word of Socrates for the intelligible form or invisible look of anything we might speak of. It is notable for its absence from this conversation; for instance, it is not mentioned in the example of mud at 147A-C, and at 147E, Theaetetus uses no noun for the one (thing) into which he gathered all the potential squares.

7   Meno especially makes this accusation in the dialogue of his name, at 80A-B. The word translated here as "unsettling" is used ordinarily to mean strange or absurd, but in this dialogue its root sense of placelessness is played on a number of times.

Have you heard that too?

Theae: I have.

Soc: Then shall I tell you the reason?

Theae: Very much so.

Soc: Just keep in mind how the whole thing having to do with midwives goes, and you will easily understand what I mean. [For you know, presumably, that none of them is midwife to others while she herself is still conceiving and bearing, but only those who no longer have the power to give birth.]

Theae: Very much so.

Soc: They say that Artemis is the reason for this, because, though she is without a mate or child, she has childbirth allotted for her protection. Now she has not therefore granted it to barren women to be midwives, [because human nature is too weak to grasp an art dealing with things it has no experience of;] but she assigned it to those who are not giving birth on account of their age, honoring their likeness to herself.

Theae: That's likely.

Soc: Then isn't this too not only likely but even necessary, that those who are pregnant and those who aren't are recognized more by the midwives than by anyone else?

Theae: Entirely so.

Soc: And surely also the midwives, by giving drugs and singing incantations, have the power either to awaken labor pangs or, if they wish, to make them milder, and also either to make those having trouble bearing give birth or, if it seems good to them when it's newly conceived to cause an abortion, they cause an abortion.

Theae: That's the way it is.

Soc: Well then, have you perceived this further thing about them, that they are the cleverest matchmakers, since they are all-around wise about discerning what sort of woman needs to have intercourse with what sort of man to give birth to the best possible children?

Theae: I don't know that at all.

E

Soc: Well, know that they take more pride in this than in cutting the umbilical cord. Consider this: do you think caring for and gathering in the fruits of the earth belongs to the same art or to a different one than recognizing what sort of plant and seed ought to be put into what sort of soil?

Theae: No, it would be the same.

Soc: But in women, dear fellow, you suppose there is one art for this sort of thing but a different one for gathering the harvest?

Theae: It's not likely, then.

150A

Soc: No it isn't. But on account of the unjust and unartful bringing together of a man and a woman, which has the name pimping, the midwives avoid even matchmaking, because they are respectable women, out of fear that they might fall under the accusation of the former by reason of the latter, even though it is proper to genuine midwives alone to engage in matchmaking correctly.

Theae: That appears so.

B

Soc: The part played by the midwives then is so great a thing, but it is a lesser one than my role. For it is not a property of women sometimes to give birth to images, while there are other times when what they give birth to is true, with this not being easy to distinguish. For if this were a property of theirs, the greatest and most beautiful work for the midwives would be to judge what is true and what is not. Don't you think so?

Theae: I do.

C

Soc: But while everything else that belongs to their art of midwifery belongs to mine, mine differs by acting as midwife to men and not to women, and by looking to their souls when they are giving birth, and not to their bodies. But the greatest thing in our art is this: to have the power to put to the test in every way whether the thinking of the young man is giving birth to something that is an image and false, or to something that is generated and true.[8] And since this at least belongs to me just as it does to the midwives, that I am barren of wisdom, and the very thing belongs to me that many people have blamed me for before now, that I question others but answer nothing myself about anything on account of having nothing wise in me, what they blame me for is true. But the cause of this is the following: the god (continually) forces me to be a midwife but (each time) prevents me from generating anything. [I myself, then, am not at all anybody wise, nor has any discovery of that sort been generated in me as the offspring of my soul.] But those who associate with me, while some of them at first appear to be entirely without understanding, all, as the association goes on, if the god permits them, improve to a wonderful extent, as it seems to them, and also to everyone else. And this is incandescently clear: that they do so despite learning nothing from me ever, but by discovering and bringing forth many beautiful things themselves out of themselves. The midwifing, however, the god and I are responsible for. This too is clear: many people before now, who didn't recognize this, and held themselves responsible while they looked down on me, either went away themselves, or were persuaded to by others, earlier than they should have. And when they had gone away they made what was left abort by bad company, and lost the things that had been midwifed by me by rearing them badly, and made more of false things and images than of what was true; and when they were finished they seemed to themselves and to everyone else to be without understanding. Aristeides, the son of Lysimachus, became one of these, as did very many others, and whenever they come back, begging for my company and carrying on wonderfully, the

D

E

151A

---

8   The words true and false in this passage are used ambiguously, but the correlation with images makes truth seem to refer here primarily to what is true-born, or truly one's own thinking.

supernatural guardian[9] that comes to me prevents me from associating with some but permits it with others, and the latter improve again. And those who associate with me also have this experience that is the same as women giving birth have: they have labor pains and are filled night and day with things they can't get through, much more than are those women, and my art has the power to awaken this sort of labor pain or to make it

B stop. Now that's the way it is for these people, but for some, Theaetetus, who in some way seem to me not to be pregnant, recognizing that they have no need of me, I very graciously make a match, and—with a god's help, let it be said—place[10] them quite adequately with those from whose company they might benefit. Many of them I have given over to Prodicus, and many to other wise and divinely inspired men.

Now I lengthened this out for you, best of fellows, on account of this: I have my suspicions that you, as you yourself also suppose, are in labor with something inside you that you are pregnant with. Offer yourself

C to me, then, as to the son of a midwife who is himself skilled at midwifery, and be eager to answer whatever I ask in whatever way you are able to. And therefore if, after I have examined any of the things you say, I deem it an image and not true and then quietly take it out and throw it away, don't go wild the way women who give birth for the first time do about their children. For many people already, you wonderful fellow, have gotten in such a state toward me that they were simply ready to bite me, whenever I would take away some nonsense of theirs, and they didn't believe

D that I was doing this out of goodwill, since they are far

---

9 The word Socrates uses is *daimonion*. At 202E of the *Symposium*, Diotima says it means something between a god and a mortal, and she calls love a thing of this kind. At 31D of the *Apology*, Socrates says that his is a sort of voice that has come to him at times since his childhood, that always prevented him from involvement in politics.

10 This word means "guess" but its root sense is hitting a place, and isn't far from the way we speak of "placing" a face. It plays here on the theme that philosophic wonder uproots us from our settled condition (see note to 149A); Prodicus of Ceos is often mentioned in the dialogues as a teacher more interested in correct use of words than in anything philosophic.

from knowing that no god has bad will toward human beings or that I don't do any such thing out of bad will either, but for me to go along with something false and conceal something true is absolutely illegitimate. So again from the beginning, Theaetetus, try to say whatever knowledge is, and never say that you are not able to, for if a god is willing and makes you manly, you will be able.

Theae: Really, Socrates, when you are so encouraging, it would be a shameful thing for anyone not to be eager in every way to say whatever he has it in him to say. So it seems to me that one who knows anything perceives that which he knows, and as it appears to me now at least, knowledge is nothing other than perception.

E

Soc: That's well said and spoken in a well-born way, my boy, for if it seems that way one needs to say so. But come on, let's examine in common whether it happens to be something generated or a wind-egg.[11] Perception is what you say knowledge is?

Theae: Yes.

Soc: It's surely no lowly statement you are running the risk of making about knowledge, but what Protagoras also used to say. But he said these same things in a somewhat different way, for he says somewhere that a human being is "the measure of all things, of the things that are, that they are, and of the things that are not, that they are not." Presumably you have read it?

152A

Theae: I have read it—many times.

Soc: Then isn't this somehow what he means, that of whatever sort things appear to me each by each, that's the sort they are for me, and of whatever sort they appear to you, that in turn is the sort they are for you, and that you are a human being and so am I?

Theae: He does mean it that way.

---

11   Defined in Samuel Johnson's Dictionary as "an egg not impregnated, an egg that does not contain the principles of life." The name is perhaps explained by the fact that such eggs float in water.

B   **Soc:** Surely it's likely that a wise man is not talking nonsense,
     so let's follow after him. Now aren't there times when,
     with the same wind blowing, one person shivers with
     cold and another doesn't? Or one does so slightly and
     another violently?

Theae: Very much so.

Soc: Well shall we say that at such a time the wind itself in
     itself is cold or not cold? Or shall we be persuaded by
     Protagoras that it's cold for the one who's shivering
     but not for the one who isn't?

Theae: That's likely.

Soc: And then also it appears that way to each of them?

Theae: Yes.

Soc: And certainly the "it appears" is a perceiving.

Theae: It surely is.

C   **Soc:** Therefore appearance and perception are the same in
     hot things too, as well as in all things of that sort. For
     whatever sort of things each person perceives them
     as, they also run a risk of being of that sort for each
     person.

Theae: That's likely.

Soc: Therefore perception is always of what is, and, being
     knowledge, is without falsity.

Theae: So it appears.

Soc: Then by the Graces, was Protagoras someone altogether
     wise who spoke in riddles like this to us, the mob of
     trash, while he was speaking the truth to his disciples
     in secret?

D   **Theae:** How do you mean that, Socrates?

Soc: I will tell you, and it's definitely no lowly statement,
     that nothing, therefore, is one thing itself by itself,
     nor could you in any way correctly call it anything
     whatever, but if you address it as large it will also
     appear small, if heavy, light, and everything at all in
     this way, since nothing is either any one thing or of

any one sort, but it's from rushing around and from motion and from blending into one another that all things come to be—we say they "are," not addressing them correctly, since nothing ever *is*[12] but is always becoming. And in this regard let all those who are wise be lined up together,[13] except Parmenides: Protagoras and Heracleitus and Empedocles, and the top-notch poets in each sort of poetry, Epicharmus in comedy and in tragedy Homer, who in speaking of

E

Ocean, progenitor of the gods with mother Tethys,

has said that all things are offspring generated out of flowing and motion. Doesn't it seem to you that this is what he means?

Theae: To me it does.

Soc: Who, then, could still have the power, when he disputed with such a great army and with its general Homer, not to become ridiculous?

153A

Theae: It's no easy thing, Socrates.

Soc: No it's not, Theaetetus, especially since these things are sufficient signs for the account that says motion produces what seems to be, that is, what becomes, while stillness produces nonbeing and perishing: heat or fire, which is what both generates and is the guardian of everything else, is itself generated out of rushing and rubbing, and these are a pair of motions. Aren't these the progenitors of fire?

Theae: These indeed.

B

Soc: And surely the generations of animals are born out of these same things.

---

12 Italics will sometimes be used for forms of the verb "to be" when they stand as complete predicates, not for emphasis but to distinguish them from the copula. This passage shows that Socrates is not using "being" to mean existence, but to mean enduring determinateness; the fleeting contents of becoming exist, since any of them is something at any place and time, but they have no being.

13 Sayings of these wise men include "everything is in flux" (Heracleitus), and "things are becoming and have no stable life" (Empedocles, fr. 26), and a line attributed to Epicharmus is "they say Chaos was the first of the gods to come to be" (fr. 1). The line from Homer is in the *Iliad*, at XIV, 201 and 302. Socrates the midwife is detecting multiple pregnancies within Theaetetus fathered on him by all these "seminal" thinkers.

Theae: How could it be otherwise?

Soc: What about this? Isn't the condition that holds[14] in bodies destroyed by stillness and inactivity, while it is kept up, for the most part, by work-outs and motions?

Theae: Yes.

Soc: And the condition that holds in the soul? Isn't it by learning and studying, which are motions, that the soul masters learnable things and keeps itself up and becomes better, while by stillness, which is lack of study and lack of learning, it understands nothing and forgets whatever it does understand?

C

Theae: Very much so.

Soc: Therefore, the good is motion, both for the soul and for the body, and contrarily?

Theae: It appears so.

Soc: Then am I to go on speaking about windlessness and calm seas and all that sort of thing, saying that stillness makes things rot and destroys them, while other things keep them safe? And must I bring in as the finishing touch to these things that the golden chain[15] Homer speaks of is nothing other than the sun, and it shows that as long as the revolving circuit and the sun are in motion, then all things are and are kept safe among gods and human beings, while if this were to stop, as though chained, all things would be destroyed and everything would come to be, as in the saying, upside down?

D

Theae: It does seem to me, Socrates, that it shows these very things that you say.

Soc: Form a conception, then, best of fellows, in this way: as for the eyes first, don't set off what you call a white

14 "The condition that holds" translates *hexis*, an active condition of holding on in a certain way. It goes past without comment here, and is dangled and pulled away by Socrates again at 197B without sparking any interest from Theaetetus. The *hexis* of the soul mentioned next becomes the general class to which Aristotle, a student of Plato, will assign knowledge (*Nicomachean Ethics* VI, 3, 1039b 31).

15 The context of this phrase, Bk. VIII, 18-27 of the *Iliad*, implies nothing like what Socrates says here. In fact it asserts the immovable supremacy of Zeus.

color as being any other thing outside your eyes, or even in your eyes, and don't even assign any place to it, for then it would presumably already be in an ordered arrangement and enduring, and would not become in becoming.

Theae: How, then?

Soc: Let's pursue the account just now being made and not set down anything as being one thing itself by itself. In this way, black and white and any other color whatever will appear to us as coming about out of the bumping of the eyes against the rushing motion that reaches them, and what we claim in each case is a color will be *154A* neither the thing bumping nor the thing bumped into, but some in-between thing that comes about privately for each. Or would you strongly swear that the way each color appears to you is the way it also appears to a dog or to any other animal?

Theae: By Zeus, not I.

Soc: What about this? Does anything whatever appear alike to another human being and to you? Is this something you hold to strongly, or is it much more the case that it's not even the same thing for you yourself, since you yourself are never holding on in a condition just like yourself?

Theae: The latter seems to me more the case than the former.

Soc: Then if that which we measure ourselves against, or which we come in touch with, were large or white or *B* hot, it would never become anything different when it ran into someone else, at least if it didn't change; and if, in turn, the thing doing the measuring or touching were each of those things, it in its turn would not become different when something else approached it or was affected by it, if it weren't itself affected. Indeed, the way it is now, dear fellow, we somehow have to say astonishing and ridiculous things handily, as Protagoras would claim, as would everyone who tries his hand at saying the same things as he does.

E (margin, top)

Theae: How? What sort of things do you mean?

C   **Soc:** Grasp a little example, and you'll know everything I want. Presumably we say that six dice, if you bring four near them, are more than the four, half again as many, while if you bring twelve, they are less, half as many,[16] and no other way of speaking can be upheld. Or will you uphold any?

Theae: Not I.

Soc: Then what if Protagoras, or anyone else, asks you: Theaetetus, is there a way that anything becomes greater or more, other than by being increased? What will you answer?

D   **Theae:** Well, Socrates, if I'm going to answer what seems the case for the thing that's in question now, I'll say that there is no way, but for the thing in question before, being on guard against saying opposite things, I'll say that there is.

Soc: Well said, by Hera, dear fellow, and in a godlike manner. But it's likely, if you answer that there is a way, that there will turn out to be something Euripidean about it, for your tongue will be unrefuted by us, but your heart will not be unrefuted.[17]

Theae: True.

Soc: Well then, if you and I were terribly clever and wise, and had closely examined all the things in our hearts, we could test each other from now on forever out of
E   our superior abundance, and joining sophistically in that sort of battle, we would bang arguments against arguments with one another. But for now, since we're

---

16   It has been noticed by commentators that six is the harmonic mean between four and twelve, since 12:4::(12-6):(6-4). The note of a six-inch string on a lyre would be a perfect fifth below that of a four-inch string, and an octave above that of a twelve-inch string. Theaetetus would know the mathematics involved, but he reveals at 206B that he thinks music is made of single notes rather than of intervals.

17   At line 612 of Euripides's *Hippolytus,* the title character threatens to violate an oath he swore with his tongue, but not with his heart, but at 656-660 he takes back the threat. It is perhaps worth noting also, in connection with Socrates's oath in this speech, that Hera speaks the line quoted in 152E as part of a deliberate lie.

common folks, we'll want first to see what the things we think are, just themselves by themselves, and whether for us they're in harmony with each other or not in any way whatsoever.

Theae: I at any rate would want to, very much.

Soc: And I too. And since that's the way it is, shall we do anything other than calmly, since we have a lot of leisure, look back over things again, not because *155A* we're acting finicky, but being genuine about closely examining our own selves and whatever these appearances in us are? The first thing we'll say in looking over them, I suppose, is that nothing could ever become greater or less, either in bulk or in number, as long as it is equal to itself. Isn't that so?

Theae: Yes.

Soc: And second, that what is neither added to nor subtracted from could never increase nor decrease, but would always be equal.

Theae: Precisely so.

Soc: And isn't there a third: that it's impossible for that *B* which was not before to be afterward without having come to be and becoming?

Theae: It seems so, at any rate.

Soc: But I suppose that these three agreed-upon things themselves do battle among themselves in our soul whenever we speak of the things involving the dice, or whenever we claim that I, being of such an age that I neither grow nor undergo anything in the opposite direction, am in the course of a year bigger than you, who are now young, and afterward smaller, when nothing has been taken away from my bulk but yours *C* has grown. For then I am afterward what I was not before, not having come to be that way, since without going through becoming a thing has no power to have become anything, and not having lost any bulk, I was never becoming smaller. And there are thousands upon thousands of other things that are this way, if indeed we accept these. I presume you're following,

Theaetetus; at any rate it seems to me that you are not inexperienced in such things.

Theae: Yes indeed, Socrates, by the gods, and it's beyond what's natural, so that I'm in a state of wonder at what in the world these things are. To tell you the truth, sometimes when I look into them I whirl around in the dark.

D   **Soc:** So, dear fellow, Theodorus appears to have placed your nature not badly, for this experience, wondering, belongs very much to the philosopher, since there is no other source of philosophy than this. And it's likely that the one who said Iris is the offspring of Thaumas[18] made his genealogy not badly. But do you understand by now why these things are this way on the basis of the things we claim that Protagoras says, or not yet?

Theae: I don't think I do yet.

E   **Soc:** Then will you be grateful to me if I join you in searching out the truth hidden away in the thinking of a famous man, or rather men, from them?

Theae: How could I not be, and very much at that?

Soc: Then look all around and see that none of the uninitiated is listening. These are the people who believe that there is nothing other than what they have the power to hold clenched in their hands, and do not accept actions or becomings or anything invisible as having any part in being.

156A   **Theae:** Surely, Socrates, you're talking about rigid and repellent human beings.

Soc: My boy, they are the very height of unrefinement, but other people, among whom are those whose mysteries I'm about to tell you, are much more sophisticated. Their starting point, on which everything we were just now saying depends, is this: that all is always motion and there's nothing else besides this, but there are two forms of motions, each infinite in multitude, the one

---

18 The genealogy is from Hesiod's *Theogony*. Iris is both the rainbow and the messenger of the gods, and her father's name sounds like the word for wonder.

having the power to act, the other to be acted upon. From the intercourse of these and their rubbing against each other there come to be offspring, infinite in multitude but twins, a perceived and also a perceiving *B* that always falls out conjoined and generated with what is perceived. Now the perceivings have names with us of this sort: seeings and hearings and smellings and coolings and burnings and, yes, pleasures and pains and desires and fears, those called by names as well as others, infinitely many without names though the named ones are vastly multitudinous. The perceived class, in turn, is of the same generation as each of these, all sorts of colors with all sorts of seeings, and sounds likewise with hearings, and the rest of the things *C* perceived coming into being co-generated with the rest of the perceivings. So what does this story mean for us, Theaetetus, in relation to the previous things? Do you take it in?

Theae: Not completely, Socrates.

Soc: Then look to see if it gets completed in some way or other. For it just means to say that all these things, as we're saying, are in motion, with speed and slowness in their motion. As much as is slow holds its motion in the same region and against the things that approach it, and so in this way it generates; but *D* the things generated in this way are faster, for they are borne away, and in being borne away they have the motion that is naturally theirs. So whenever an eye, with anything else of the same measure with it that approaches it, generates a whiteness and a sensing born jointly with that, which latter things could never have come to be if either of the former ones had come up against anything else, at the time when the seeing from the eyes and the whiteness from the thing that *E* jointly begets the color are being borne off between them, thereupon the eye becomes full of seeing and just then sees, and becomes not in any way a seeing but a seeing eye, while the thing that co-generated the color is filled to overflowing with whiteness, and becomes in turn not whiteness but white, either a white stick or stone or whatever sort of thing happens to get colored

157A

with such a color. And so the other things, hard and hot and all the rest, must be conceived in the same way, that none is anything itself by itself, the very thing we were saying at one time, but in mutual intercourse all things come into being and come to be of all sorts from their motion, since to think of what's active and what's passive among them as being something particular in any one case is, as they assert, not possible in any fixed way. For there isn't even any active thing until it comes together with what's passive to it, or any passive one until it comes together with what's acting on it, and the thing that comes together with one thing and acts comes to sight again as being acted upon when it comes up against something else. And so, out of all these things, there is the very thing we were saying from the beginning, that there is no one thing itself by itself, but always a becoming for someone, and *being*

B

must be rooted out from all quarters, despite the fact that we have been forced many times, and just now, by custom and our lack of knowledge, to use it. But one ought not, according to the statement of the wise men, to go along with this, not with a something or a someone's or a mine or a this or a that, or with any other name that makes anything stand still; but one ought, in accordance with nature, to utter the names becomings and acted upons and perishings and alterings, since if anyone makes anything stand still by his speech, the one who does this is easily refuted. And one needs to speak this way both part by part and about many things gathered together, on any which

C

gathering people place as a name "human being" or "stone" or each animal and form.[19] So, Theaetetus, do these things seem pleasing to you, and would they be satisfying to your taste?

Theae: I don't know, Socrates, and I'm not able to get a notion about you either, whether you are saying what seems so to you or trying me out.

Soc: You aren't remembering, dear fellow, that I neither

---

19   This is the third occurrence in the dialogue of the word *eidos*. (See note to 148D.) It was used to begin the revelation of the mysteries in 156A, by gathering motions into two forms with different powers or potencies.

know any such thing nor make them out to be mine, but I am barren of such things[20] and I'm midwifing you, and for the sake of this I'm chanting incantations and administering doses of each of the wise things for you to get a taste of, until I pull out into the light, together with you, your own opinion. Once it has been pulled out I'll examine whether it will show up as a wind egg or as something generated. So be confident and perseverant and answer in a good manly way whatever appears to you in connection with the things I ask about. *D*

Theae: Ask away.

Soc: Then tell me again whether you're satisfied that there is not anything good and beautiful and all the things we were going through just now, but always becoming.

Theae: Well to me anyway, when I'm listening to you going all through it this way, it appears wonderfully to have sense in it, and that one ought to conceive it in the very way in which you've gone over it.

Soc: Then let's not leave out how much is left out in it. It *E* leaves out what has to do with dreams and diseases, both other sorts and insanity, and everything that is called mishearing or mis-seeing or any other sort of misperceiving. For presumably you know that in all of these cases, by general agreement, the account we're going through right now is held to be refuted, on the grounds that in them more than anything, *158A* false perceptions come about for us, and those things that appear to each person are far from being so, but altogether to the contrary, nothing of what appears is so.

Theae: Most true, Socrates, what you say.

Soc: Then what argument is left, my boy, for the one who sets down perception as knowledge, and that those things that appear to each person are so for that one to whom they appear?

20   This passage suggests that Socrates's barrenness at his time of life is just the fact that he is no longer confused about whether an opinion he finds in himself is his own.

Theae: Socrates, I shrink from telling you that I don't have it in me to say, because you jumped all over me just now for saying that, though to tell you the truth I wouldn't have the power to dispute that those who are insane or dreaming are holding false opinions whenever they suppose themselves to be gods or think in their sleep that they have wings and are flying.

B

Soc: Then you aren't aware of just such a dispute about them, and especially about dreaming and being awake?

Theae: What sort?

Soc: What I suppose you've heard many times when people ask what distinguishing mark anyone could have to demonstrate by, if someone were to ask now, like this at present, whether we're asleep and dreaming all the things we are thinking or whether we're awake and having a waking conversation with each other.

C

Theae: Really, Socrates, it's a stumper by what distinguishing mark one ought to show it, since all the same things follow along step for step as in a choral dance.[21] For nothing prevents our seeming in sleep to be discussing with each other what we were discussing just now, and when while dreaming we seem to be narrating dreams, the likeness of the latter and the former is unsettling.

Soc: So you see, at any rate, that the disputing is not difficult, when it's also disputed whether that disputing is made awake or in a dream, and since the time during which we're asleep is equal to that during which we're awake, in each of the two our soul contends combatively that the seemings that are present to it at every time are true more than anything, so that for one equal time we claim that it's these things that have being, and for the other equal time that it's those, and we insist just as strongly in each case.

D

Theae: Most absolutely.

---

21 Literally, an antistrophe, in which a chorus, or matching half-chorus, dances the steps of a preceding stanza (the strophe) with their left-right directions reversed. In the next sentence, Theaetetus's mathematical bent gives this mirror-image situation a twist that suggests an infinite oscillation.

Soc: Then the same argument also applies to diseases and states of insanity, except for the time, since it's not equal?

Theae: Correct.

Soc: Then what? Is what's true going to be determined by the plenitude or scarcity of time?

Theae: That would surely be plentifully ridiculous.   *E*

Soc: But do you have any other clear marker at all to show which sorts of these opinions are true?

Theae: It doesn't seem to me that I do.

Soc: Hear from me, then, what sorts of things would be said about them by those who determine that the things that seem so at every time are true for the one they seem that way to. They speak in the following way, as I am supposing it, asking "Theaetetus, when something is different in every respect, could it have in any respect the same potency as the thing it's different from? And let's not conceive of the thing we're asking about as being in some way the same but in another way different, but as wholly different."

Theae: In that case it's powerless to have anything about it that's the same either in potency or in any other respect   *159A* whatever, when it's just precisely different.

Soc: Then isn't it also necessary to agree that such a thing is unlike?

Theae: It seems that way to me.

Soc: Therefore, if anything happens to become like or unlike anything, either itself or anything else, we'll say that in being made alike it's becoming the same, but in being made unlike it's becoming different?

Theae: Necessarily.

Soc: And weren't we saying before that the active things would be many and infinite, and the same way for the things acted upon?

Theae: Yes.

Soc: And of course that when one of them mixes together with one thing and with another, it will generate not the same things but different ones?

B   **Theae:** Entirely so.

Soc: So from now on let's talk about me and you and everything else in accordance with the same account, as Socrates keeping healthy or in turn as Socrates getting sick. Shall we say the latter is like or unlike the former?

Theae: Now this "Socrates getting sick," do you mean this as a whole in relation to that whole "Socrates keeping healthy"?

Soc: You conceive it beautifully. I mean that very thing.

Theae: Then presumably unlike.

Soc: And therefore he's different in just this very way that he's unlike?

Theae: Necessarily.

Soc: And so with sleeping, and with all the things we were
C   just now going through, you'll say the same?

Theae: I will.

Soc: Then each of the things that are of such a nature as to act on something else, when it catches a Socrates keeping healthy, will treat me as one thing, but when getting sick, as something different?

Theae: How's it not going to?

Soc: And so in each case I, the thing being acted upon, and that thing acting will generate different things?

Theae: What else?

Soc: So whenever I drink wine while keeping healthy, it will appear pleasant and sweet to me?

Theae: Yes.

Soc: And that's because, from the things we agreed to
D   before, the thing acting and the thing being acted upon generate a sweetness and a perceiving, both

borne off together, and the perceiving, being from the side of the thing being acted upon, fills up the tongue with perceiving, while the sweetness, borne around it from the side of the wine, makes the wine both be and appear sweet to the tongue that's keeping healthy.

Theae: The earlier things were agreed on by us entirely in that way.

Soc: But whenever it catches me getting sick, first of all, in truth, it doesn't catch the same person, or is it any otherwise than that? For surely it comes to someone unlike.

Theae: Yes.

Soc: So, in turn, this sort of Socrates and the drink of wine   *E* paired up generate different things, around the tongue a perceiving of bitterness and around the wine a bitterness coming about and being borne away, while the wine becomes not a bitterness but bitter and I become not a perceiving but something perceiving?

Theae: Precisely.

Soc: Then I'll never come to be perceiving anything else in the same way, for a perceiving of something else is a different perceiving, and makes the perceiving thing   *160A* be of a different sort and something else; nor will the thing acting on me ever come to be of the same sort by coming together with something else and generating the same thing, since it will come to be of a different sort by generating something different from something different.

Theae: These things are so.

Soc: And neither will I come to be of the same sort as myself, nor that thing the same sort as itself.

Theae: Certainly not.

Soc: But it is a necessity, at any rate, that whenever I come to be perceiving, I come to be perceiving something, since there is no power for something perceiving to come to be perceiving nothing; and it's for that thing to come   *B* to be for someone, whenever it comes to be sweet or bitter or anything of the sort, since there is no power to become sweet but sweet for no one.

Theae: Absolutely.

Soc: So what's left, I suppose, is that we be for one another, if we are, or become for one another, if we're becoming, since indeed necessity binds together our very being, though it binds it together with no other thing nor does it even bind either of us ourselves together. So we're left bound up together with one another, so that if anyone names anything, either as being or as becoming, it's necessary for him to say it is or comes to be for someone or belonging to someone or relative to someone. But that there's anything itself in itself, either being or becoming, one must not either say oneself or accept when anyone else says it, as the account we've gone through indicates.

C

Theae: Absolutely, Socrates.

Soc: So then since the thing acting on me is for me and not for anyone else, don't I and not anyone else perceive it?

Theae: How could it be otherwise?

Soc: Therefore my perceiving is true for me, since it always belongs to my being, and I am the judge, in accord with Protagoras, of the things that are for me, that they are, and of the things that are not, that they are not.

Theae: That seems likely.

D

Soc: How, then, if I am without falsity and do not slip in my thinking about beings and becomings, could I not be a knower of the very things of which I'm the perceiver?

Theae: There's no way you could not.

Soc: Therefore it was stated very beautifully by you that knowledge is nothing other than perception, and there has been a falling in together to the same result of what comes from Homer and Heracleitus and all that sort of tribe, that all things are in motion like streams, and from the most wise Protagoras, that a human being is the measure of all things, and from Theaetetus, that since these things are so, perception becomes

E

knowledge. Well, Theaetetus, are we going to say that this is your newborn child, as it were, and what I have midwifed? What do you say?

Theae: Necessarily so, Socrates.

Soc: Well then, it seems that at last we have generated this, whatever it happens to be. And after its birth for its christening[22] it must truly be run around in a circle by our talk when we examine it, so that it won't escape our notice if what is coming into being is not worth rearing, but is a wind-egg and false. Or do you think *161A* that just because it's yours it ought to be reared in any case and not put away, or will you bear up under seeing it cross-examined, and not get violently angry, like a woman with her first-born, if someone quietly takes it away from you.

Theo: Theaetetus will bear up under it, Socrates; he's not touchy about anything. But in the sight of the gods, tell us! Can it still be that it's not this way?

Soc: You are a lover of arguments, anyway, Theodorus, naively so, and a simple soul if you suppose that I am some bag of arguments, easily coming out with one to say "On the other hand, these things aren't that way." But you aren't aware of what's happening, that none of *B* the arguments comes out of me, but they always come out of the person conversing with me; I know nothing more than a trifling amount, enough to get an account out of someone else who's wise and to accept it in a measured way. And now I will try to get this one out of this fellow here, not saying anything myself.

Theo: That's a more beautiful thing, Socrates, as you say. Do it that way.

Soc: Do you know, then, Theodorus, what I wonder at your companion Protagoras about?

Theo: What sort of thing? *C*

---

22   The Athenian naming ceremony was called the *Amphidromia*, or running-around, and the baby was carried around the hearth in the presence of the assembled family, friends, and household gods.

Soc: The other things he has said are very pleasing to me, that what seems to each person also is that, but I'm in a state of wonder at the beginning of his discourse, that when he began the *Truth* he didn't say "a pig is the measure of all things," or a dog-faced baboon, or some other more outlandish thing that has perception, in order that he might have begun to speak to us magnificently and with complete contempt, displaying that while we were in wonder at him as at a god for his wisdom, he happens, after all, to be

D   no better off in intelligence than a little round frog, not to mention any other human being. How can we say otherwise, Theodorus? For if whatever he might hold as an opinion by perceiving will be true for each person, and no one else will discern another person's experience any better than he, nor will anyone be more authoritative in examining the opinion than anyone else, as correct or false, but as has been said many times, each person himself will form his opinions alone about his own experience, and these are all correct and true, how in the world, companion, was Protagoras wise,

E   so as to consider himself worthy of being a teacher of others, justly charging high fees, while we were more lacking in understanding and had to go to school to him, though each one is himself the measure of his own wisdom? How can we not say that Protagoras was saying these things to sway the crowd? As for me and what belongs to my art of midwifery, I am silent about how much ridicule we deserve, as I suppose does the whole serious practice of conversation. For to examine the appearances and opinions that belong to one another and try to refute them, when what belongs

162A to each person is correct—isn't that a lot of resounding bubble-headedness if the *Truth* of Protagoras is true, and he wasn't playing with us when he made his utterances from the holy of holies of his book?

Theo: Socrates, the man was a friend, as you said just now. So I wouldn't take kindly to Protagoras's being refuted by my agreeing, nor on the other hand to resisting you contrary to my opinion. So take Theaetetus again; anyway, he appeared just now to be very much in tune with you in his answering.

Soc: And if you went to Sparta, Theodorus, to the wrestling-   *B*
gyms, would you think you had the right to look at
the other people naked, some of them in bad shape,
and not strip down yourself to display your form in
return?

Theo: Well what do you think I'd do if they were going
to leave it up to me and take my decision? Just as I
suppose I'm going to persuade you now to let me look
and not drag me into the gym when I'm already rigid,
but to wrestle with the one who is younger and more
flexible.

Soc: Well, Theodorus, if that's the way you like it, I won't   *C*
hate it, as the people who like proverbs say. So one
has to go back to the wise Theaetetus. And tell us first,
Theaetetus, in connection with the things we were just
now going through, are you too in a state of wonder
when you're brought to light so suddenly as being no
worse in wisdom than any human being or even any
god? Or do you suppose the Protagorean measure is
any less to be said about gods than about humans?

Theae: By Zeus, I don't. And I'm very much in wonder at
this very thing you're asking. For all the time we were
going through the way they said that what seems so to   *D*
each person also is that way for the one it seems so to,
it appeared to me that what was said was very good,
but now it has instantly fallen over to the opposite
way.

Soc: It's because you're young, dear boy, and so you are
quick to pay attention to and be persuaded by talk
that sways the crowd. For Protagoras, or someone
else on his behalf, will say in response to these things:
"You well-born children and old men, you're the
ones talking for the crowd as you sit there together
dragging gods into the middle of things, even though I
banish them from being spoken or written about—that   *E*
they are or that they are not—and you say the things
that most people would approve of hearing, that it's a
terrible thing if each human being isn't going to be any
different in wisdom from any sort of livestock. But you
don't give any demonstration at all or say anything

that's necessary, but you use what seems likely, even though if Theodorus or any other geometer wanted to use that to do geometry, he wouldn't be worth a single solitary thing. So you and Theodorus consider whether you're going to accept persuasive talk and what seems likely in arguments that speak of such great things."

163A

Theae: Well it isn't just, Socrates; neither you nor we would say so.

Soc: So it seems likely that one must look at it in a different way, according to what you and Theodorus say.

Theae: In an altogether different way.

Soc: So let's look in the following way, to see, therefore, whether knowledge and perception are the same or different. For presumably all our talk was straining toward that, and for the sake of that we set in motion these many unsettling things. Isn't that so?

Theae: Absolutely.

B

Soc: Then should we in fact agree that all those things that we perceive by seeing or by hearing are also known at the same time? For example, before we understand the language of foreigners, should we say either that we don't hear it when they utter it, or that we both hear and know what they say? Or if, in turn, we don't know the letters of the alphabet, but we're looking at them, should we strongly insist either that we don't see them, or that we know them if we do see them?

Theae: We should say, Socrates, that we know just that very thing that we see and hear, in the one case that we see and know the shape and the color, and in the other case that we hear and at the same time know the high and low pitch; but what the reading teachers and language interpreters teach about them, we should say that we neither perceive by sight or hearing nor know.

C

Soc: That's the very best, Theaetetus, and it's not worth it to dispute with you about that, so that you may still grow.[23] But look at this other thing that's coming at us, and see how we'll repel it.

Theae: What sort of thing now?

Soc: This sort: if someone were to ask, "Is it in one's power, with anything one has ever become a knower of, and still has and keeps a memory of that very thing, that there could ever be a time when he remembers but does not know this very thing that he remembers?" I'm being wordy, it seems, but all I want to ask is whether one who's learned something doesn't know it if he remembers it.

D

Theae: How could that be, Socrates? What you say would be a monstrosity.

Soc: So I'm talking nonsense, maybe? But look: don't you say that to see is to perceive and sight is perception?

Theae: I do.

Soc: So then one who has seen something has become a knower of that which he has seen, according to what's been said right now?

E

Theae: Yes.

Soc: Then what? Don't you speak of memory, of course, as something?

Theae: Yes.

Soc: Memory of nothing or of something?

Theae: Certainly of something.

Soc: Isn't it of things one has learned and things one has perceived, of some sorts of things like that?

Theae: What else?

---

23   In what sense can Theaetetus's answer be the best, yet still admit of dispute and growth? It seems to have the precision and correctness characteristic of mathematics, but still to miss the most important thing, the difference between "knowing" a page of foreign writing that one cannot read and knowing what it means. In this example there is a surface that is perceived, but it seems to be pregnant with something knowable.

Soc: And what someone has seen, presumably he sometimes remembers?

Theae: He remembers.

Soc: Even with his eyes shut? Or does he forget when he does that?

Theae: That would surely be a terrible thing to claim, Socrates.

164A **Soc:** It's necessary, however, if we're going to keep what was said before. If we don't make this claim, that's swept away.

Theae: I suspect so too, by Zeus, but I'm not getting it sufficiently; tell me how.

Soc: In this way: one who sees, we are saying, has become a knower of that very thing which he sees, since sight and perception and knowledge are agreed to be the same thing.

Theae: Entirely so.

Soc: But one who sees and has become a knower of what he has seen, if he shuts his eyes, remembers it but is not seeing it—right?

Theae: Yes.

B **Soc:** But "is not seeing" means "does not know" if in fact sees means knows.

Theae: True.

Soc: Therefore, it follows that what someone has become a knower of and still remembers, he does not know since he is not seeing it—the very thing we were saying would be a monstrosity if it were to come about.

Theae: What you say is most true.

Soc: So something impossible appears to result if one claims that knowledge and perception are the same.

Theae: It seems so.

Soc: Therefore one must say that the two are different.

Theae: They run that risk.

Soc: Then what could knowledge be? It seems that one must
say that again from the beginning. And yet, Theaetetus,
what in the world are we getting ready to do?   C

Theae: About what?

Soc: We appear to me to be crowing like a badly begotten
rooster before it's won a fight, when we've jumped off
the argument.

Theae: How's that?

Soc: In a spirit of contradiction, we seem to have gotten
an agreed conclusion by agreeing about words, and
to be satisfied when we've gotten the upper hand in
the argument by some such means, and though we
claim we're not competitive but philosophic, we are,   D
without being aware of it, doing the same things as
those terrible men.

Theae: I still don't understand how you mean that.

Soc: Then I'll try to make clear exactly what I'm thinking
about it. We asked whether someone who has learned
and remembers something doesn't know it, and having
demonstrated that one who has seen and has his eyes
shut is remembering but not seeing, we demonstrated
that he was not knowing but at the same time was
remembering, and this is impossible. And so in this
way Protagoras's story was destroyed, and at the same
time so was yours about knowledge and perception,
the one that said they're the same.

Theae: So it appears.   E

Soc: It wouldn't have happened, I suppose, dear fellow, if
the father of the other story were alive, but he would
be fighting off the danger in many ways; but here we
are, flinging mud on the orphan itself, and not even
the guardians whom Protagoras left behind, of whom
Theodorus here is one, want to come to its aid. We're
in danger of having to come to its aid ourselves, for the
sake of what is just.

165A **Theo:** That's because it's not I, Socrates, but instead Callias the son of Hipponicus, who's guardian of the things that belonged to him. Ourself, for some reason or other, turned away sooner from bare words to geometry, and yet we'd be grateful to you anyway if you come to its aid.

Soc: Beautifully said, Theodorus. So take a look at my aid, for one would agree to things more terrible than the ones right now before us if he did not turn his attention to the words by means of which we're accustomed, for the most part, to affirm and deny. Shall I speak to you in any way, or to Theaetetus?

B **Theo:** To us in common, then, but let the younger one answer; he'll be less disgraced if he's tripped up.

Soc: Then I ask you the most terrifying question. It is, I suppose, something like this: "Is it possible for the same person, while knowing something, not to know the thing that he knows?"

Theo: So, what do we answer, Theaetetus?

Theae: Presumably that it's not in his power, I suppose.

Soc: Not if you're going to set down seeing as knowing. For how will you deal with an inescapable question, when you've got yourself stuck in a well, as the saying goes, and a man who's not to be knocked off course asks you, as he holds his hand over one of your eyes, whether you see his cloak with the eye that's blocked?

C

Theae: I suppose I'll say, not with that one but certainly with the other one.

Soc: Then you're seeing and not seeing the same thing at the same time?

Theae: In a certain sense that's so.

Soc: That's not at all what I'm setting up, he'll say, and I didn't ask you in what sense, just whether what you know, you also don't know. And now you obviously see what you don't see, and you've agreed precisely that seeing is knowing and not seeing is not knowing. So from these things, deduce what follows for you.

Theae: Well, I deduce that things are opposite to what I set   *D*
down.[24]

Soc: And perhaps, you wondrous fellow, you would have
suffered through more of the same if someone had
asked in addition whether there is knowing that's
sharp and that's dull, and knowing near but not far,
and knowing the same thing vigorously and slightly,
and thousands of other things that a light-infantry-
style man fighting as a mercenary with words would
be asking while lying in ambush, ever since you set
down knowledge and perception as the same, and
bombarding hearing and smelling and perceptions
like that, and he would have kept on refuting,   *E*
attacking and not letting up until, wondering at his
much-prayed-for wisdom, you were tied up hand and
foot by him; and when he had gotten the better of you
and chained you up, from then on it would be about
ransom—how much money was resolved on by you
and him. Now perhaps you might say "Well, what sort
of speech will Protagoras call up as a relief force for
his own side?" Shall we do anything other than try to
state it?

Theae: Let's try by all means.

Soc: Well, there are all these things that we're saying in   *166A*
defending him, and also I suppose, with contempt for
us, he'll close in on the same thing, saying "This simple
Socrates, when he frightened some little boy by asking
him whether it's possible for the same person at the
same time to remember and not know the same thing,
and the frightened boy denied it, because he didn't
have the power to see ahead, made me look ridiculous
in his speeches. But, you most lackadaisical Socrates,
it's like this: whenever you examine anything of mine

---

24   The present argument thus has the formal structure of a *reductio* proof in
mathematics. That is suggestive in many directions, since (a) rejecting various
claims about knowledge may amount to a demonstration of a possibility that
isn't considered, (b) Theaetetus's use of the general word "opposite" rather than
the precise word "contradictory" might reveal a tendency to jump to the opposite
extreme when something is seen to be false, and (c) if the formal correctness of
this argument does not make it convincing, something might be lacking when
the mathematician's way of reasoning is applied to philosophic questions.

B

by questioning, if the one who's asked is tripped up after answering with just exactly the sort of things I would answer, then I am refuted, but if he answers with other sorts of things, the one who was asked is himself refuted. To start with, do you think anyone would go along with you that a memory that's present to him of things he experienced, when he's no longer experiencing them, is an experience of the same sort as he underwent at the time? It's far short of it. Or, next, that anyone would shrink from agreeing that it's possible for the same person to know and not know the same thing? Or even if he was afraid of this, that he'll ever grant that one who's becoming unlike is the same person he was before becoming unlike? More than that, do you think he'll grant that this person is a "him" and

C

not a "them", with these becoming infinite, if in fact a process of becoming unlike is going on—that's if he's really going to need to be on guard against getting caught in the words going back and forth? But, you blessed one," he'll say, "go up against the very thing that I say in a way more suited to a well-born man, if you have the power to, and prove that perceptions do not come privately to each of us, or that even though they do come privately, what appears would nonetheless not come about for each person alone—or if it has to be called "being," that it would not "be" for just the one to whom it appears. So when you talk about a pig or a dog-faced baboon, not only are you being pig-ignorant yourself, you also carry over the people who hear you to act this way toward my writings, which is

D

no beautiful thing to do. I declare that the truth holds as I have written it, since each of us is a measure of the things that are and are not, and yet we differ one from another in thousands of ways for this very reason, that to one person some things are and appear, to another person others do. And far from denying that there is wisdom and a wise man, I say that very person is wise who, for any one of us to whom bad things appear and are, makes them change over into appearing and being good things. So don't go hounding the discourse again

E

for my wording, but learn still more clearly what I mean, in this way: recall the sort of thing that was in what

was said before, that to the one who's sick, what he eats
appears and is bitter, while to the one who's healthy
the opposite is and appears. Now there's no need to
make either of them wiser, and one doesn't even have   *167A*
the power to, nor should one accuse the sick person of
being lacking in understanding because he has such an
opinion, while the healthy one is wise because he has
a different sort, but one should produce a change from
one to the other, since that other is a better condition to
be holding in. In this way in education too, one should
produce a change from one condition that holds to a
better one, but while a doctor produces a change with
drugs, a sophist[25] does so with speeches. One does not,
however, make someone who's been having some false
opinion afterward have some true opinion, for there
is no power to have as opinions either things that are
not, or other things besides those one experiences,
and the latter are always true. But I suppose that   *B*
when someone with a burdensome condition holding
in his soul has opinions akin to his own condition, a
serviceable condition would make him have different
opinions, of that sort, which latter appearances some
people, from inexperience, call true, but I call the one
sort better than the other, but not at all truer. And far
from calling wise people frogs, dear Socrates, when
they have to do with bodies I call them doctors and
when they have to do with plants I call them farmers;
for I claim that the latter induce in plants, in place of
burdensome perceptions, whenever any of them are   *C*
sickly, serviceable and healthy perceptions and truths,
and that wise and good rhetoricians make serviceable
things, instead of burdensome ones, seem to cities to be
just. Seeing as how whatever sorts of things seem just
and beautiful to a city are those things for it so long as
it considers them so, it's the wise man who, in place
of each sort of things that are burdensome for them,
induces serviceable things to be and seem so. And by
the same account, the sophist who has the power to
train in this way those who are being educated is both

---

25 The word "sophist" was in bad odor, at least among the Athenians (see, e.g., *Meno*
91C-92C and *Protagoras* 312A), but Protagoras claimed that title openly and proudly,
with no pretense at teaching any particular skill (Protagoras 318 D-E, 349A).

D wise and deserving of a lot of money from those who get educated. Thus it's the case both that some people are wiser than others, and that no one has false opinions, and also that you, whether you like it or not, have to hold still for being a measure, for in these ways, this account is saved. Which, if you have it in you to dispute it from the beginning, dispute it then, by going all the way through an account to replace it. But if you want to dispute it by asking questions, dispute it by asking questions, for this account is not something one ought to run away from, but for anyone who has any sense, it

E most of all things ought to be chased after. Just do it this way: don't be unjust in your questioning. For in fact it's a big-time irrationality for someone who claims to care about virtue to do nothing else but keep on being unjust in the things he says. And it is being unjust in such a situation whenever anyone doesn't keep it separate when he's spending his time being competitive, and separate when he's having a conversation, and in the former he may be playful and trip people up as much as he has the power to, but in having a conversation he should be serious and help the person he's conversing with back upright again, pointing out to him only those

168A stumbles in which he himself has been knocked off his feet by himself and by his previous associations. Now if you do this, those who spend their time with you will hold themselves responsible for their own confusion and helplessness, and not you, and they'll pursue you and love you, but hate themselves and run away from themselves to philosophy, in order to become different people and be set free from what they were before. But if you do the opposite of these things, as most people do, the opposite result will follow for you, and you'll

B make your associates show themselves as haters of this business instead of philosophers when they become older.[26] So if you're persuaded by me of what was also said before, then in no hostile or combative way, but

---

26 Recall what Theodorus said at 165A about his own association with Protagoras. Compare also the history of a certain Antiphon, who once associated with a disciple of Zeno and Parmenides, as reported at *Parmenides* 126C-127A. This counterfeit Protagoras seems to suggest testing philosophic teachers by seeing whether they generate philosophic lives in their associates.

having come down in your thinking to join with me as gracious men, you'll truly examine what we mean when we declare that all things are in motion and that whatever seems so also is that way, both for each private person and for each city. And from these things you'll go on to examine whether knowledge and perception are the same or different, but not as you did just now on the basis of customary phrases and words, which most *C* people, when they drag them around any which way at random, hold out as all sorts of insoluble difficulties for one another." With these things, Theodorus, I have come to the aid of your companion as much as is in my power, small aid from small power, but if he himself were alive, he would have helped out the things that belong to him more mightily.

Theo: You are being playful, Socrates; you came to the man's aid with the full vigor of a young man.

Soc: That's nice of you to say, my companion. And tell me: you took it in just now, I'm sure, when Protagoras was talking and scolding us because, in making our *D* arguments to a little boy, we were contesting what belonged to him by means of the boy's fear, and he cast aspersions on what we were doing as some sort of charming display of wit, while he was being solemn about the measure of all things, and he called on us to be serious about his discourse?

Theo: How could I not take it in, Socrates?

Soc: Well then, do you urge that we be persuaded by him?

Theo: Strongly.

Soc: Well, you see that everybody here except you is a young boy, so if we're going to be persuaded by the man, it's necessary for you and me, by questioning and answering each other, to take his discourse seriously, *E* so that he won't have this to accuse us of, at least, that we examined his discourse by being playful with youngsters.

Theo: What? Isn't it certain that Theaetetus would follow the argument better as it's being thoroughly examined than many men who have long beards?

Soc: But not any better than you, at least, Theodorus. So don't suppose that I have to defend your dead companion in every way and you in none. Come on then, best of fellows, follow a little way, just until that point at which we know whether, as a consequence, there's a need for you to be a measure about geometrical diagrams, or whether everybody, alike with you, is sufficient to himself in astronomy and the rest of the things about which you're given the credit for surpassing others.

169A

Theo: It's not easy, Socrates, while sitting beside you, not to give an account, and I was talking nonsense just now when I claimed you'd allow me not to strip down, and wouldn't force me the way the Spartans do; but you seem to me to go more in the direction of Sciron, since the Spartans demand that one go away or strip down, but you seem to me to act a part more fitting for some Antaeus,[27] since you don't let anyone go who comes near you until you force him to strip down and wrestle in speeches.

B

Soc: In the best possible way, Theodorus, you've painted an image of my disease; I, however, am more stubborn than those others. For already Heracleses and Theseuses by the thousands, strong in their speaking, have met up with me and bashed me good and well, but I don't stand down any the more for all that, so terrible a lust has gotten into me for work-outs over these things. So don't you begrudge me a rubbing up against each other to benefit yourself and me at the same time.

C

Theo: I'm not contradicting you any more; just lead wherever you want. In any case, I've got to endure the fate you've spun for me about these things by being cross-examined. It won't, however, be possible for me to hold myself out to you any further than what you've proposed.

Soc: Even up to that point is enough. And watch out very

---

27 Sciron was a mythical highway robber who liked to push his victims off a cliff. Antaeus was a giant born from the earth by the sea god; he was an unbeatable wrestler as long as he was in contact with the earth. Theseus defeated the former, and Heracles the latter.

carefully for me for this sort of thing: that we do not anywhere without noticing it make any of our statements in a playful form and have someone scold us for it again.

D

Theo: I'll certainly try at any rate, as much as I have the power to.

Soc: Then first, let's get hold of this again just where we had it before, and see whether we were correctly or incorrectly disdainful of the account when we found fault with it because it made each person self-sufficient in intelligence. Even Protagoras went along with us that some people surpass others about what is better and worse, and that they are in fact wise, didn't he?

Theo: Yes.

Soc: Then if he himself were present and agreeing to it, instead of our going along with it on his behalf to help him out, there would be no need to take it back up again and establish it, but now perhaps someone might hold that we have no authority for an agreement on his behalf. For this reason it would be more beautiful to make our agreement about this very thing more clear, since it causes no small shift for it to be this way or some other.

E

Theo: What you say is true.

Soc: Then not by means of any others but out of his own statement, let's get the agreement by the briefest possible means.

170A

Theo: How?

Soc: Like this: he says, presumably, that what seems so to each human being also is that way for the one to whom it seems that way?

Theo: Indeed he does say that.

Soc: Well then, Protagoras, we're also stating opinions[28] of a human being, or rather of all human beings, and

---

28 The Greek word for opinion (*doxa*) has the same root as that for seeming (*dokein*).

claiming that no one at all does not consider himself wiser than others in some respects and other people wiser than himself in other respects, and in the greatest dangers at least, when people are in distress in military campaigns or diseases or at sea, they have the same relation to those who rule them in each situation as to

B   gods, expecting them to be their saviors, even though they are no different from themselves by any other thing than by knowing; and all human things are filled with people seeking teachers and rulers for themselves and for the other animals, as well as for their jobs, and in turn with people who suppose themselves to be competent to teach and competent to rule. And in all these situations, what else are we going to say but that human beings themselves consider there to be wisdom and lack of understanding among them?

Theo: Nothing else.

Soc: Then do they consider wisdom true thinking and lack of understanding false opinion?

C   **Theo:** What else?

Soc: Well, Protagoras, how are we going to treat the statement? Are we going to claim human beings always hold true opinions, or sometimes true ones and sometimes false? From both claims, surely it follows that they do not always hold true opinions but both sorts. So consider, Theodorus, whether any of the people surrounding Protagoras, or you yourself, would want to insist pugnaciously that there's no other person who considers anyone else to be lacking in understanding or to hold false opinions.

Theo: It's just not a believable thing, Socrates.

D   **Soc:** And yet by necessity the statement asserting that a human being is the measure of all things comes down to this.

Theo: How's that?

Soc: Whenever you, having judged anything on your own, declare an opinion about it to me, then according to his account, let this be true for you; but isn't it possible for us others to become judges of your judgment, or do we always judge that you hold true opinions? Or do thousands of people on each occasion who hold opposite opinions do battle with you, regarding you as judging and believing false things?

Theo: By Zeus, Socrates, that's right, many thousands,[29] as Homer says, and they're the ones who cause the troubles I have with human beings.

E

Soc: Well then, do you want us to say that at that time you hold an opinion that's true for yourself but false for the thousands?

Theo: It appears from the account anyway that that's necessary.

Soc: And what about Protagoras himself? Isn't it necessary, if neither he himself, nor most people, were to believe that a human being is a measure, as in fact the others don't, that what he wrote is the truth for no one? But if he himself did believe it, while the multitude do not share his belief, you know that first of all, however many more there are to whom it doesn't seem so than there are to whom it does, then it is not so by that much more than it is.

171A

Theo: Necessarily, if indeed it's going to be and not be so according to each opinion.

Soc: This next point is the most exquisite subtlety it has in it: he goes along with the belief about his own belief of those who hold the opposite opinion, by which they consider him to be saying something false, since presumably he agrees that the things all people hold as opinions are true.

Theo: Very much so.

Soc: Then he'd be going along with calling his own belief false, if he's agreeing that the belief is true of those who consider him to be saying something false?

B

---

29   Theodorus adds an adverb to produce what has been called the minimum possible quotation from Homer, a routine vague exaggeration used in the *Odyssey* at XVI, 121, XVII, 422, and XIX, 78.

Theo: Necessarily.

Soc: But the others do not go along with saying that their own opinions are false?

Theo: No indeed.

Soc: And he agrees again that even that opinion is true, from what he has written.

Theo: It appears so.

C

Soc: Therefore, from everybody starting from Protagoras, there will be a dispute, but by him instead there will be an agreement, whenever he goes along with it that someone who says the opposite is holding a true opinion, and then Protagoras himself will be agreeing that neither a dog nor any random human being is a measure about any single thing that he doesn't understand. Isn't that so?

Theo: It's so.

Soc: Then since it is disputed by everyone, the *Truth* of Protagoras will be true for no one, not for anyone else and not even for him himself.

Theo: We're running down my companion too much, Socrates.

D

Soc: But really, my friend, it's unclear whether we're also running past what's correct. It seems likely, therefore, that he, being older, would be wiser than we are, and if suddenly, right here, he would pop out his head as far as the neck, once he'd refuted me in many ways for speaking nonsense, which is likely, and you for agreeing, having sunk back, he'd be swept off and running away.[30] But for us, I suppose, it's necessary that we make use of ourselves, of whatever sort we are, and always say those things that seem so. And so, now too, should we say anything other than this: that anyone at all would agree that one person is wiser

---

30 The description suggests the image of perception Socrates made, beginning at 156A. The apparition of Protagoras's disembodied head is a fleeting instance of becoming.

than another, and also that one is more lacking in understanding than another?

Theo: It seems so to me, at any rate.

Soc: And does it seem to you also that the account stands up most of all in that aspect in which we sketched it *E* when we were coming to the aid of Protagoras, that the way most things seem is also the way they are for each person, things that are hot, dry, sweet, and everything of that type, while if he'd go along with it anywhere that one person surpasses another in any respects, he'd be willing to say, in connection with what's healthy and diseased, that not every woman and child and even animal is competent to cure itself by recognizing what's healthy for itself, but here, if anywhere, one person surpasses another?

Theo: That's the way it seems to me.

Soc: And then, too, about political things, whatever sorts of *172A* things each city supposes are beautiful or shameful, just or unjust, holy or not holy, and sets down as lawful for itself, these also are that way in truth for each, and in these things no private person is any wiser than any other, nor is any city wiser than any other; but in setting down what's advantageous or disadvantageous for itself, here again, if anywhere, he'd agree both that one advisor surpasses another and that the opinion of one city surpasses that of another in relation to truth, and he'd hardly have the daring to say that whatever *B* a city sets down as advantageous for itself, supposing it to be so, is also what will be advantageous to it beyond any question. But in that realm I was speaking of, among the things that are just and unjust or holy and unholy, people are willing to insist strongly that there are not any such things by nature, having their own being, but instead that what seems so to people in common becomes true at that time, whenever it seems so and for as long as it seems so. At any rate, those who would not completely say what Protagoras says regard wisdom in some sort of way like this. But Theodorus, an argument coming out of an argument, a greater one out of a lesser, is catching up with us. *C*

Theo: Well, aren't we at our leisure, Socrates?

Soc: We appear to be. And while I've certainly noticed it often at other times, you surprising fellow, still I'm seeing even now how likely it is that people who've spent a lot of time among philosophies[31] are manifestly ridiculous as rhetoricians when they go into the law courts.

Theo: How do you mean?

Soc: Those who've bounced around in courts and such places from their youth run the risk, compared with those who've been reared in philosophy and that sort of pastime, of being raised like menial servants as against free men.

Theo: How, exactly?

Soc: In this respect: just what you were talking about, leisure, is always present for the latter, and they conduct their discussions in peace at leisure. Just as we're taking over one argument that's come out of another, now already a third,[32] so do they if the one that comes up is more satisfying to them than the one that's in front of them, as it is to us. And it's of no concern to them whether they talk in long speeches or short ones, if only they hit upon what *is*. But the others are always talking in an unleisured way, since flowing water is sweeping them along,[33] and there's no room for making speeches about whatever they desire, but the opposing party in the lawsuit stands there holding necessity and an outline of the case that's read out at them, outside the bounds of which one may not speak. Their speeches are always about a fellow slave, in front of a sitting slavemaster who has some sort of lawsuit

---

31   According to Seth Benardete, this is the only place Plato ever uses this word in the plural.

32   The last transition occurred at the end of 171C, from a purely logical refutation of Protagoras's statement to a consideration of situations to which it might apply and not apply. It's not clear whether the third argument is the one now coming up about the philosophic life, or the one that follows it, beginning in 177C.

33   A water clock limited the times of speeches in court, but in this dialogue flowing water has also been an image of fleeting things, as opposed to what *is*.

in his hand, and their competition is never varying but always about that very thing, though often the race is for one's life; as a result of all this, they become *173A* intense and sharp—knowing how to fawn on their master in words and worm their way into his favor by deeds—but small and not upright in their souls, for the slavery they've been in since youth has taken away their growth, straightness, and freedom, forcing them to do crooked things by piling great dangers and fears on their still tender souls, which they don't have the power to hold up under by means of anything just and true, but turning directly to what's false and to returning injustice to one another they get bent and *B* battered many times over, so that they end up out of adolescence as men who have nothing healthy in their thinking, though they've become dreadfully clever and wise, as they suppose. So that's the sort these people are, Theodorus, but are you in favor of our going through our choral group, or shall we let them go and turn back to the argument, so that we don't abuse too much the thing we were just now talking about, our freedom and changeability in the things we talk about?

Theo: By no means, Socrates; I'm for going through it. For you have put it very well that we who belong in this *C* kind of chorus are not subordinate to the arguments, but instead the arguments are like servants of ours, and each of them waits on us, to be finished whenever that seems good to us, since no judge is set up over us, and not even a spectator, as with the playwrights, to criticize and govern us.

Soc: Well then, let's speak, since, as it appears, that's what seems good to you, about those who head the chorus, for why would anyone speak about those who pass their time in philosophy poorly? And first, presumably, from their youth, these people don't know the way to *D* the marketplace, or where the courthouse or council chamber is, or any other place of public assembly of the city, and laws and things voted on, spoken or written, they neither see nor hear, and as for the zealous efforts of political parties for offices, and their meetings and dinners and celebrations with flute girls, not even in their dreams does it occur to them to have anything to do with them. And whether anyone in the city has been born well or badly, or has any taint that has come from his ancestors on either the paternal or maternal side, is something he no more notices than the proverbial

E   drafts of water in the sea. And all these are things that he doesn't even know that he doesn't know, since he's not holding off from them for the sake of being well thought of, but in his being, only his body has its place and makes its home in the city, while his thinking, considering all these things as little or nothing, deems them worthless in every respect and takes flight, as Pindar says, "underneath the earth," treating its surfaces geometrically, "and above the heavens," engaged in

174A   astronomy, searching out in every way the nature of each and every one of the beings as a whole and not lowering itself at all to any of the things nearby.

Theo: How do you mean this, Socrates?

Soc: In the same way, Theodorus, that when Thales[34] was engaged in astronomy and looking upward and fell into a well, a certain elegantly witty Thracian maidservant is said to have made fun of him, saying that he was eager to know the things in the heavens but couldn't notice what was in front of him right at his feet. The same joke holds good when applied to all

B   those who spend their lives in philosophy. For in his very being, such a person is unaware of his next-door neighbor, not only unaware of what he's doing but little short of unaware of whether he's a human being or some adopted changeling; but what a human being is, and what's appropriate for such a nature, as distinct

---

34   Thales of Miletus was one of those the Greeks spoke of as the seven sages. The others were more famous for political wisdom, and Thales was often considered the first philosopher. This story links up with Socrates's remark in 155D that the only beginning of philosophy is wonder, to suggest that philosophic wonder is an experience in which the ground drops away from beneath one's feet, and familiar ways of thinking and explaining things cannot be relied on. Since Thales claimed that the origin of all things is water, he fell into his own first principle. He gained fame by predicting the solar eclipse of 585 BC, and wealth by cornering the market on olive-presses when astronomical evidence led him to expect a favorable harvest.

from the rest, to do or have done to it, he inquires into
and keeps up his efforts to investigate. I'm sure you
understand, Theodorus—or don't you?

Theo: I do, and what you say is true.

Soc: That's exactly why such a person, my friend, getting
together with anyone in private or in public, just   C
as I was saying at first, whenever he's forced, in a
courtroom or anyplace else, to discuss the things at his
feet and in front of his eyes, provides a laugh not only
for Thracian girls but also for the rest of the crowd, as
he falls into wells and into every sort of helplessness
by his inexperience, and his lack of good form is
terrible, as he brings on himself the reputation of being
good for nothing. For in exchanges of mockery he has
nothing of his own to mock anyone with, because he
knows no evil about anyone, from not having cared
about that, so being at a loss he appears ridiculous; and   D
in exchanges of praise and boasts by others, when it
becomes obvious that he's laughing not as a pretense
but in his very being, he's thought to be an idiot. For
when a tyrant or king is having praises heaped on
him, he thinks he's hearing one of the herdsmen, like
a pig-herder or a shepherd or some cowhand, being
congratulated for milking a lot of cattle, though he
considers that they're herding and milking an animal
that's more discontented and treacherous than those
others, and that it's necessary for such a ruler to become
no less crude and uneducated than the herdsmen from   E
his lack of leisure, with a wall enclosing him like an
animal pen on a mountain. And whenever he hears
that someone possessing ten thousand acres of land,
or still more, has possessions wonderful in extent,
it seems to him that he's hearing about a very small
amount, since he's accustomed to looking at the whole
earth. Or when they sing the praises of their families,
saying that someone is well-born for having seven
rich ancestors to point to, he considers the praise to be
coming from people whose vision is completely dulled
and short-sighted, since from lack of education they   *175A*
don't have the power to look to the whole of eons and
figure out that everyone has had countless thousands

of ancestors and forefathers, among whom, for anyone at all, there have been many thousands of rich men and beggars, and kings and slaves, both barbarian and Greek, so when people become pompously solemn over a list of twenty-five ancestors, tracing it back to Heracles the son of Amphitryon, it makes its absurdity

B   plain to him by its pettiness, and since the twenty-fifth ancestor up from Amphitryon was of whatever sort chance happened to make him, as was the fiftieth ancestor up from him, he laughs at those who are unable to figure it out and get rid of the emptiness of a soul with no intelligence. So in all these cases, such a person is laughed at by most people, for being stuck up about some things, as it seems, as well as for being ignorant of the things at his feet, and for being at a loss in each particular situation.

Theo: What you're saying, in absolutely every detail, is what happens, Socrates.

Soc: But, my friend, whenever he himself drags someone

C   upward, anyone who is willing, with him, to get past his "What injustice am I doing to you or you to me?" and into an examination of justice and injustice themselves, of what each of the pair is and in what respect they differ from everything else or from each other, and to get past "whether it's a king who's happy, or also someone who has gold"[35] to an examination about kingship, and human happiness and misery in general, what sort of thing the pair of them is and in what way it's appropriate by nature for a human being to get hold of the one of them and get away from the other—when on all these subjects it's

D   necessary in turn for that fellow who's small in soul and sharp and lawyerly to give an account, then he gets his turn for payback as he dances to the opposite tune.[36] Dizzied from being suspended up high and looking down from above in mid-air, distressed at

---

35   The wording of this question varies in the manuscripts, and editors have tried various emendations, but the only important thing about the question is its unimportance.

36   Literally, to give or pay back the antistrophe; see the note to 158C.

the unfamiliarity of it, helpless and stammering, he doesn't provide a laugh to Thracian girls, or to anyone else who's uneducated, since they don't perceive it, but to all those who've been brought up in a manner opposite to that of slaves. This is the way that belongs to each, Theodorus, one of them nurtured in his very being in freedom and leisure, the one whom you call a philosopher,[37] who's blameless for seeming to be naive and of no account whenever he stumbles into slavish services, such as not knowing how to pack up a bed-roll, or how to sweeten up a sauce or flattering talk, while the other in his turn is capable at performing all such services keenly and sharply, but doesn't know how to throw his cloak over his right shoulder like a free man, or, for that matter, how to sing hymns in the right way to the life of gods and of happy men by getting the things he says into harmony.

E

176A

Theo: If you could persuade everyone of what you say, Socrates, as you persuade me, there would be more peace and fewer evils among human beings.

Soc: But it's not possible for evils to be done away with, Theodorus, since it's necessary that there always be something contrary to what's good, nor is it possible for evils to be situated among the gods, but they make the rounds of the mortal nature and of this place here. That's in fact the reason it behooves one to try to get away from here to there as quickly as possible, and getting away is becoming like a god as far as is in one's power, while becoming like a god is becoming just and holy with intelligent judgment. For surely, you best of fellows, it's not at all an easy thing to persuade people that the end for the sake of which most people say one ought to avoid vice and pursue virtue is therefore not that for the sake of which one should practice the one and not the other, namely in order that one might seem to be good and not bad; this, as it appears to me, is the babbling of old women, as the saying goes. Let us speak the truth, in this way: a god is in no respect

B

---

37   It is noteworthy that many of the attributes given to this person would not apply to Socrates, who held himself above petty politics but not above all political life.

C unjust in any way, but is just in the maximum possible sense, and there is no one more like him than whoever among us becomes in his turn as just as possible. And the true cleverness of a man, or his nothingness and unmanliness, have to do with this, for the recognition of this is true wisdom and virtue, and ignorance of it is blatant stupidity and vice, while the other things that seem to be cleverness and wisdom, when they come along involved in political power, are degraded, and in

D the arts they're debased. So with someone who's being unjust and saying or doing unholy things, it's the best thing by far not to go along with saying that he's clever in his shamelessness, since they delight in the reproach, and believe they're hearing that they're not lightweights, useless burdens on the earth,[38] but men of the sort one needs to be to stay safe in a city. So one needs to tell the truth, that they're the sort of people they think they're not, all the more so because they think they're not, for they're ignorant of the penalty for injustice that they ought least to ignore. It's not what it seems to them to be, beatings and executions,

E which people who do no injustice sometimes suffer, but a penalty one has no power to escape.

Theo: What do you mean?

Soc: That there are patterns, my friend, established in the very being of things, of the divine as most happy and of the godless as most miserable, but not seeing that this

177A is how it is, through their folly and utter senselessness, these people are unaware that they are making themselves like the latter by their unjust actions, and unlike the former. So they pay the penalty for it by living a life in the image of what they've become like, but if we say to them that, unless they get rid of their cleverness, even when they're dead that place that's unsoiled by evils will not receive them, but they will always hold in themselves the likeness of their way of life, evil joined in living with evil, they, since they're clever and shameless in every way, will hear these

---

38 An allusion to Homer, an epithet applied in mockery to Odysseus at XX, 379 of the *Odyssey*, and in self-reproach by Achilles to himself at XVIII, 104 of the *Iliad*.

things as coming from some sort of senseless people.

Theo: Very much so, Socrates.

Soc: I surely know it, my companion. One thing, however, *B*
does turn out to be the case with them: whenever in
private they have to give an account and get one back
about the things they object to, and they're willing in
a manly way to stick with it for a long time and not
run away in unmanly fashion, at such a time, you
strange man, they themselves end up unsettled and
dissatisfied with themselves in connection with the
things they're saying, and that rhetorical skill of theirs
somehow withers away, so that they seem no different
from children. Now about these things, since they
happened to be spoken of as side-issues, let's stand
back—if we don't, more will be constantly flowing in *C*
and be a burial mound over our original discussion—
and let's go back to the previous things, if that also
seems good to you.

Theo: To me, Socrates, it's no more disagreeable to listen to
things like this, since they're easier for someone who's
my age to follow. However, if it seems good, let's go
back.

Soc: Well then, we were just about at that place in the
discussion at which we were saying about the people
who claim that the being that's carried along also *is*,
and the thing that at any time seems so to each person
also is so, for that one to whom it seems so, that they
wanted to insist strongly in other situations, and not
least about what's just, that more than anything, *D*
whatever a city sets down as seeming just for itself
also is just for the city that sets it down, for as long
as it's set down, but that in the case of what's good,
no one would still be so manly to dare to fight it out
that whatever a city sets down supposing it to be
advantageous for itself also is advantageous for so
much time as it's set down, unless someone would just
give it that name; but that would be a travesty of what
we're talking about, wouldn't it?

Theo: Certainly.

E　**Soc:** For it's not the name that one needs to talk about, but the thing named that one needs to look into.

Theo: No indeed.

Soc: But whatever this is the name of, surely that's what a city aims at in its lawmaking, and it makes all its laws as advantageous as possible to itself to the extent it supposes them so and has the power. Or does it engage in lawmaking by looking to anything else?

178A　**Theo:** Not at all.

Soc: And then does it always hit what it aims at, or does each city also often completely miss its target?

Theo: I certainly think they also miss their targets.

Soc: Well then, everyone would agree to these same things still more from the following perspective, if someone were to frame the question about the entire form in which the advantageous also happens to be, and that, presumably, is what has to do with a future time. For whenever we engage in lawmaking, we set down the laws on the grounds that they will be advantageous in a later time, and we would correctly call this the "future."

B　**Theo:** Certainly.

Soc: Come on then, let's question Protagoras, or any of the others who say the same things he does, in the following way. "A human being is the measure of all things," as you people say, Protagoras, of white things, heavy things, light things—there's nothing whatever of that sort that he's not the measure of—for since he has the seat of judgment for them in himself, and supposes them to be of whatever sort he experiences, he supposes them to be true for him and to be for him. Isn't that so?

Theo: It's so.

Soc: And about the things that are going to be in the future,
C　Protagoras, we'll say, does he have in himself the seat of judgment for them, and whatever sort of things he believes are going to be, do these also come to be

for that one who believes in them? For instance heat: whenever any ordinary person believes that he himself is going to get a fever, and that this sort of heat is going to be present, and someone else, a doctor, believes the opposite, in accordance with which one's opinion shall we say the future is going to turn out? Or will it be in accord with that of both, and to the doctor he won't become hot or feverish, but to himself he'll be both?

Theo: That would certainly be funny.

Soc: But I suppose about the sweetness or dryness that's going to be present in wine, the opinion of the grower, and not that of the harpist, is authoritative.   *D*

Theo: What else?

Soc: And in turn about what's going to be dissonant and what's going to be consonant, a gym teacher wouldn't have a better opinion than a musician, when afterward, even to the gym teacher himself it will seem to be consonant.

Theo: By no means.

Soc: Then too, when a banquet is being prepared, the judgment of someone unskilled at cooking who's going to be a guest at the feast, about the pleasure there's going to be, is less authoritative than that of a gourmet cook. About the pleasure there already is   *E* for each person, or that there already has been, let's not yet do battle with the account, but about how things will seem and how they're going to be for each person in the future, is he himself the best judge? Or are you, Protagoras? At least about what's going to be persuasive to each of us in speeches in a courtroom, would you have a better opinion beforehand than any ordinary person whatever?

Theo: Very much so, Socrates; in that very thing he used to swear emphatically that he surpassed everyone.

Soc: By Zeus, that's so, my dear man, or else no one would have conversed with him, giving him a lot of money for   *179A* it, if he didn't persuade his associates that no prophet or anyone else could judge better than he what was going to be and to seem to be so in the future.

Theo: Most true.

Soc: So then acts of lawmaking as well as what's advantageous have to do with the future, and everyone would agree that it's necessary when making laws for a city often to fail to attain what's most advantageous?

Theo: Very much so.

B

Soc: Therefore it's a measured response from us to your teacher that it's necessary for him to agree both that one person is wiser than another and that such a person is a measure, while for me, who lacks knowledge, to become a measure is not necessary in any way whatever, as the argument on his behalf was just now forcing me to be, whether I wanted to or not.

Theo: In that way especially the argument seems to me to be caught out, Socrates, and it's also caught out in this way, in that it makes the opinions of everyone else authoritative, while these opinions were shown to hold that his statements are not true at all.

C

Soc: In many another way, Theodorus, the claim that every opinion of everyone is true could be caught out, at least in such a form, but about the present experience of each person—and it's out of these that perceptions and the opinions resulting from them come—it's more difficult to catch it out as not being true. But perhaps I'm not making any sense, and it may turn out that they're things that can't be caught out, and those who claim that they're both obvious and kinds of knowledge could perhaps be saying things that are the case, and Theaetetus here was not off-target in his assertion

D

when he set down perception and knowledge as the same thing. So one must approach it more closely, as the speech on behalf of Protagoras kept demanding, and by knocking on that sort of being that's carried along, one must examine whether it has a solid ring to it or sounds cracked; then too, a battle has come up about it, no low-level one and among no few people.

Theo: It's far from being low-level, and it's making

tremendous headway all around Ionia, for the companions of Heracleitus lead the chorus for this kind of talk very mightily.

Soc: For that reason, you see, dear Theodorus, one must examine it all the more and from the beginning, in just the way they elaborate it.   *E*

Theo: Absolutely so. In fact, Socrates, about these Heracleitean things, or as you say, Homeric and still more ancient, it's no more possible to discuss them with those people around Ephesus who claim to be well-versed in them than with those maddened by a stinging gadfly. They're simply carried away, just like the things they write about, and as for standing still for an argument or for a question and calmly answering   *180A* and asking in turn, there's less of that in them than none at all, and "none at all" is not too much of an exaggeration for the not even a little bit of calmness that's to be found in these men. But if you ask any of them anything, they pull out cryptic little sayings like arrows from a quiver and shoot them off, and if you inquire about this to get an explanation of what's been said, you'll be struck by another one, newly rephrased. You'll never get any conclusion from any of them, nor for that matter do they themselves from each other, but they're on guard very carefully to allow nothing to be stable, neither in speech nor in their own souls, since, I   *B* suppose, they'd consider that being static. Against that they're in a state of total war, and as much as they have the power to, they drive it out from everywhere.

Soc: Perhaps, Theodorus, you've seen these men fighting, but haven't been with them when they're at peace, since they aren't companions of yours. But I imagine they reveal that sort of thing at leisure to their disciples, whom they want to make like themselves.

Theo: What sort of disciples, you strange fellow? Among such people one does not become another's disciple;   *C* they sprout up spontaneously, wherever each of them happens to get his inspiration, and the one regards the other as knowing nothing. Now what I was going to say is that you could never get an account from these people whether they were willing or unwilling, but we need to take it over ourselves, in order to investigate it like a geometrical proposition.

Soc: That's a measured response, anyway. But now this proposition that we've taken upon ourselves, is it anything other than the one we've gotten from the

D ancients, who concealed it from most people with poetry, that the flowing streams Ocean and Tethys happen to be the genesis of all other things and nothing stands still, and from the latter-day people who, because they're wiser, declared it openly, so that even shoemakers would understand their wisdom once they'd heard it and stop foolishly believing that some things stand still and others are in motion, but having learned that all things are in motion they would honor those who declared it? But I nearly forgot, Theodorus, that other people in their turn proclaim things opposite to what these say.

E Since it is wholly motionless, being is the name
for the all,[39]

and all the other things that many a Melissus and Parmenides strongly insist on in opposition to all these folks, that all things are one and it stands still in itself, having no place in which it moves. How shall we treat all these people, my companion? For in going forward little by little, we haven't noticed that we've fallen into

181A the middle between both sides, and if we don't get away somewhere by defending ourselves, we'll pay the penalty in the way people do who play "over the line" in the gyms, when they've been caught by both sides and are pulled in opposite directions. Now it seems to me that one ought to examine the others beforehand, the ones on whom we've made a start, the flowing ones, and if they show themselves to be making sense, we'll help them ourselves to drag us over with them, and try to get away from the others; but if the ones who bring the whole to a standstill seem to us to be saying truer

---

39 This verse resembles line 38 of fragment VIII of Parmenides, but with more words wrong than right. This has given scholars fits (see, e.g., Taran, *Parmenides*, pp. 133-136), but Socrates seems not so much to be misquoting as engaging in free variation on a theme.

things, we'll flee instead to them, away from those who **B**
set motionless things in motion. But if both sides show
themselves to be saying nothing within measure, we'll
be laughed at if we consider ourselves to have anything
to say, since we're lowly folks who'd be rejecting very
ancient and thoroughly wise men as unqualified. So,
Theodorus, see whether there's anything to gain by
going forward into such a great danger.

Theo: But it's not acceptable at all, Socrates, *not* to examine
thoroughly what both groups of men say.

Soc: One would be obliged to examine them, since you are
so eager. It seems to me, then, that the starting point **C**
for an examination about motion is: what sort of thing
are they talking about when they say that all things are
in motion? I mean to say something like this: are they
talking about some one form of it, or, as it appears to
me, two? However, don't let it seem that way only to
me, but you too take a share in it with me, so that we'll
undergo in common anything there's a need for. And
tell me, do you call it moving whenever something
changes from place to place or even turns around in
the same place?

Theo: I do.

Soc: Then let this be one form. But whenever something is
in the same place, but gets old, or becomes black from **D**
white or hard from soft, or alters by any other sort of
alteration, isn't it worth declaring that a different form
of motion?

Theo: It's necessary, in fact.

Soc: Then by two forms of motion I'm speaking of this pair,
alteration and change of place.

Theo: And speaking correctly.

Soc: Accordingly, now that we've divided this in that way,
let's now have a discussion with those who claim
all things are in motion, and ask: do you claim that **E**
everything is in motion in both ways, being carried
around and altering, or one thing in both ways and
another thing in one of the two?

Theo: By Zeus, I have no way to say, but I suppose they'd claim both ways.

Soc: If they don't, anyway, my companion, it will appear to them that things are both moving and standing still, and it will be no more correct to say that all things are in motion than that all things are standing still.

Theo: What you say is most true.

182A   **Soc:** Then since it's necessary for them to be in motion, and for there not to be any not-moving present in anything, all things always have to be moving with all motions.

Theo: Necessarily.

Soc: Then consider for me this claim of theirs: about the becoming of hotness or whiteness or whatever, weren't we saying that they claim something of this sort, that each of these is carried along together with a perceiving, between something acting and something acted upon, and that the thing acted on becomes perceptive, though not a perception, while the thing acting comes to be of a certain sort, though not a certain-sortness? Now perhaps the word "certain-sortness"[40] seems to be a barbarism, and you don't understand what's being

B   stated all at once, so listen to it described part by part. The thing acting is neither hotness nor whiteness but becomes hot or white, or the rest in the same way, for you surely remember that we were speaking that way in the things we said before, that since nothing is one thing itself by itself, neither in turn is the thing acting or the thing acted upon, but from the coming together of both with each other, they bring forth the perceivings and perceiveds, the latter becoming of certain sorts and the former coming to be perceiving.

Theo: I remember; how could I not?

C   **Soc:** Then let's let the rest go, whether they speak of it in some other way or in this one, and let's be on guard

---

40   This word could be translated as "quality," and is used occasionally by both Plato and Aristotle as an artificial substitute for the more direct word that means "of a certain sort." It is formed out of that latter word and a noun suffix, parallel to hotness and whiteness.

only for this, for the sake of which we're speaking, and ask: All things, as you claim, are in motion and flux, is that so?

Theo: Yes.

Soc: Then are they in both the kinds of motions that we distinguished, being carried along and altering?

Theo: How could they not, if indeed they're to be wholly in motion?

Soc: Then if they were only carried along and didn't alter, we would presumably have a way to say what sorts of things are in flux, namely the ones being carried along. Or how do we mean it?

Theo: That way.

Soc: But since not even this stays still, that it's the flowing white that's flowing, but it's changing, so that even of this itself—of the whiteness—there's a flux, and a change into another color, in order that it may not be caught staying still in this way, is it ever possible to address it as any color so as to give it a name correctly?

D

Theo: What contrivance could there be, Socrates, or for that matter, for any other such thing, if indeed it's always slipping out from under the one who's speaking, inasmuch as it's in flux?

Soc: And what are we to say about perception of any sort whatever, such as about seeing or hearing? Does it ever stay still as just seeing or hearing?

E

Theo: It shouldn't, at any rate, if all things are in motion.

Soc: Therefore one must not attach the name of seeing to it any more than not seeing, nor of any other sort of perception more so than not, if all things are in motion in all ways.

Theo: Certainly not.

Soc: And yet perception is knowledge, as both I and Theaetetus were saying.

Theo: That was so.

Soc: Therefore, when we were asked what knowledge is, we answered no more about knowledge than about non-knowledge.

183A **Theo:** You appear to.

Soc: A beautiful correction that would turn out to be by us of our answer, when we were eager to demonstrate that all things are in motion, just in order for that answer to show itself correct. But as it seems, it showed that if all things are in motion, every answer, no matter what one is answering about, is equally correct, in claiming that it's this way or not this way—or, if you wish, becomes, in order that we not stop them in our speech.

Theo: What you say is correct.

Soc: Except, Theodorus, that I said "this way" and "not this way," but one ought not even to say "this way," since *B* "this way" would no longer be in motion, nor in turn "not this way," for that is not a motion either, but those who state this account ought to establish some other utterance, since now at least they have no words for their own hypothesis, unless perhaps "no way" might therefore fit best for them, since it means nothing definite.

Theo: They'd be most at home with that sort of slang anyway.

Soc: Well then, Theodorus, we've gotten rid of your companion, and we'll no longer go along with him *C* that every man is a measure of all things, if he's not someone sensible; and we won't go along with it that knowledge is perception, at least not along the path of all things' being in motion, unless Theaetetus here says otherwise in any way.

Theo: That's the best thing you've said, Socrates, for when these things were finished, I too was obliged to be rid of answering you, according to our agreement,[41] since

---

41   Offered in 169A and accepted in 169C, but what is remarkable is that Socrates has found a way to set Theodorus's various motives for resisting philosophy against one another to make him find that he has a stake in the outcome of a philosophic inquiry in spite of himself.

what pertained to Protagoras's account has reached its end.

Theae: No, Theodorus, not until you and Socrates go over   **D**
those who claim on the other hand that the all stands
still, as you just now proposed.

Theo: Though you're young, Theaetetus, are you teaching
your elders to be unjust by transgressing agreements?
Just prepare yourself for how you'll give Socrates an
account of the things that are left.

Theae: If that's what he wants. But I would have taken
the greatest pleasure in hearing about the people I'm
speaking of.

Theo: You're calling out "horsemen into a plain" when you
call out Socrates into arguments. Just ask and you'll
hear.

Soc: But I think, Theodorus, at least about what Theaetetus
is urging, that I'm not going to obey him.   **E**

Theo: But why exactly won't you obey?

Soc: While I'm ashamed that we might examine in a crude
way Melissus and the others who say the all is one,
standing still, I'm less ashamed of that than I am before
one being: Parmenides. Parmenides appears to me to
be, in the words of Homer, "an object of reverence to
me" and at the same time "terrifying."[42] For when I
was very young and he was very old I mixed in with
the man, and to me he appeared to have something   ***184A***
deep about him that was completely true-born. So I'm
afraid that we won't understand what was said, and
that we'll be left much further behind what he was
thinking when he said it, and my greatest fear is for
that for the sake of which our discussion was set going,
about what knowledge is, that it may go unexamined
under the impetus of arguments rushing in to join the
party, if anyone lets them have their way. This is so
both for other reasons and because what we're now
waking up is inconceivable in extent; if one examines

---

42   These two adjectives are combined twice in the *Odyssey*, but this precise wording
occurs only in the *Iliad*, at III, 172, applied to Priam by Helen.

it as a side-issue, it would be treated in an unworthy manner, and if one examines it adequately, it will lengthen out to hide the question about knowledge from sight. We ought not to do either one, but try to relieve Theaetetus, by the art of midwifery, of the things he's pregnant with about knowledge.

Theo: Well, if it seems that way to you, that's what we ought to do.

Soc: Now then, Theaetetus, consider this much still further about what's been said: you answered that knowledge is perception, didn't you?

Theae: Yes.

Soc: So if someone were to question you in this way, "With what does a human being see white and black things, and with what does he hear high and low tones?" I suppose you'd say "with eyes and ears."

Theae: I would.

Soc: An easy acceptance of words and phrases that does not make a precise scrutiny of them is in most cases a sign that one is not ill-bred, but instead the opposite of this is ungenerous, but there is a time when it is necessary, just as it's necessary now to catch up the answer you gave, insofar as it's not correct. For consider: which answer is more correct, that it's the eyes with which we see, or through which we see, and the ears with which we hear, or through which we hear?

Theae: Through which we perceive, in each case, it seems to me, Socrates, rather than with which.

Soc: Yes, I suppose it would be a terrible thing, my boy, if many senses were sitting in us as in wooden horses, but they didn't all converge into some one look, whether it's the soul or whatever one ought to call it with which we perceive whatever is perceived, through these as though they're implements.

Theae: It seems to me it's that way rather than the other.

Soc: Well, it's for this following reason that I'm being so precise with you about them: is it with something of

ourselves that's the same that we reach, through the
eyes, white and black things, and through the rest, in
turn, some other things, and will you have the ability,
when you're questioned, to trace all such things back
to the body? But perhaps it's better for you to speak
when you're asked these things, rather than for me to
meddle on your behalf. So tell me, with hot things and
hard things and light things and sweet things, don't
you set down those things through which you perceive
each sort as belonging to the body? Or do they belong
to something else?

E

Theae: Nothing else.

Soc: And will you also be willing to agree that those things
you perceive through a different power are incapable
of being perceived through another one, such as those
through hearing, through sight, or those through sight,
through hearing?

185A

Theae: How could I not be willing to?

Soc: Therefore, if you think anything about both together,
you couldn't be perceiving anything about both
together through the one organ, or in turn through the
other.

Theae: No, I couldn't.

Soc: Now first, about sound and about color, do you think
this very thing about both, that the pair of them *is*?

Theae: I do.

Soc: Then too that each of them is other than the other and
the same as itself?

Theae: What else?

B

Soc: And that both together are two, but each is one?

Theae: That too.

Soc: And do you have the power to examine whether the
pair are unlike or like each other?

Theae: Maybe.

Soc: But through what do you think all these things about the pair of them? For it's not possible either through hearing or through sight to grasp what's common about them. And this is a further piece of evidence about what we're saying: if it were in one's power to examine them both as to whether the pair is salty or not, you know you'll have the capacity to say what you'd examine them with, and that is obviously neither sight nor hearing but something else.

Theae: How could it not be a certainty that it's the power through the tongue?

Soc: Beautifully said. But now what is the power through that reveals to you what's common to all things as well as to these, to which you attach the names "is" and "is not" and whatever we were just now asking about that applies to them? What sort of organs will you allot to all these, through which what is perceptive in us perceives each sort?

Theae: You're talking about being and not-being, and likeness and unlikeness, and what's the same and other, and also about one and the rest of number having to do with them. And it's clear that you're also asking, about the even and the odd, and as many other things as follow along with these, through which of the things that belong to the body we perceive them with the soul.

Soc: You're following superlatively well, Theaetetus, and it's about these very things that I'm asking.

Theae: Well by Zeus, Socrates, I at least would have no way to say, except that it seems to me there's absolutely no such special organ for these things as there is for those others, but the soul itself, through itself, appears to me to observe the common things involved in all things.

Soc: Because you are beautiful, Theaetetus, and not ugly as Theodorus was saying, for one who speaks beautifully is beautiful and good. And in addition to being beautiful you did me a favor by sparing me a very long speech, if it's apparent to you that there are some things the soul itself observes through itself and others through powers that belong to the body. For this was

what seemed so to me about it, and I wanted it also to
seem that way to you.

Theae: Well, it surely is apparent.   *186A*

Soc: Then among which sort do you place being? For this
most of all follows closely upon everything.

Theae: I place it among the things the soul itself, by itself,
reaches out for.

Soc: And the like and the unlike and what's the same and
other?

Theae: Yes.

Soc: Then what about beautiful and ugly and good and
bad?

Theae: It seems to me that it's the being of these as well that
it looks to, especially in their relations to one another,
gathering up[43] in itself the past and present things in   *B*
relation to the future ones.

Soc: Hold it. Won't it perceive the hardness of what's hard,
and likewise the softness of what's soft, through
touch?

Theae: Yes.

Soc: But their being, and that the pair of them is, and their
oppositeness to each other, and in turn the being of
oppositeness itself, the soul itself, by going back over
them and comparing them to one another, tries to
judge for us.

Theae: Very much so.

Soc: Aren't some things present by nature for both human
beings and animals to perceive right from birth, all   *C*
those experiences that stretch through the body to the
soul, while other things, gathered up about these in

---

43   "Gathering up" translates *analogizesthai*; its meaning extends from reckoning up
the result of a calculation to making or perceiving analogies. This rich word that
Theaetetus comes up with out of himself is a promising start toward articulating
the way knowing happens in mathematics, and it is picked up by Socrates in his
third following speech. It may be noted that Theaetetus fails to gather this thought
into the answer he gives in 187A, which determines the rest of the dialogue.

connection with their being and advantageousness, come to be present with difficulty and over time, through many troubles and through education, to those to whom they come to be present at all?

Theae: Absolutely so.

Soc: Is it possible, then, for someone who doesn't even reach being to reach truth?

Theae: It's out of one's power.

Soc: And will anyone ever be a knower of that about which he fails to reach the truth?

D   **Theae:** How could he, Socrates?

Soc: Therefore, knowledge is not present in the experiences, but in the process of gathering together what's involved in them, for in the latter, as it seems, there is a power to come in touch with being and truth, but in the former there is no power.

Theae: So it appears.

Soc: Then will you really call the former and the latter the same thing, when the pair of them has such great differences in it?

Theae: It wouldn't be just, at any rate.

Soc: So what name do you give to the former, the seeing, hearing, smelling, feeling cold, feeling hot?

E   **Theae:** Perceiving, I'd say; what else?

Soc: In total, then, you call it perception?

Theae: Necessarily.

Soc: And it, we're saying, has no share in coming in touch with truth, since it doesn't with being either.

Theae: No, indeed it hasn't.

Soc: Nor, therefore, has it any share in knowledge.

Theae: No, it hasn't.

Soc: Therefore, Theaetetus, perception and knowledge could not ever be the same thing.

Theae: It appears not, Socrates; and it has now become most obvious that knowledge is different from perception.

Soc: But it was not at all for the sake of this that we began discussing it, to find out what knowledge is not, but what it is. Nevertheless, we've made this much progress at least, that we won't look for it in perception at all, but in that name, whatever it is, that the soul has when it occupies itself, by itself, with beings. *187A*

Theae: Well that, at any rate, Socrates, as I suppose, is called having opinion.

Soc: You're correct about supposing it, dear fellow. But look again now, from the start, once you've wiped away all the previous things, and see whether you observe anything more, since you've come forward to this point, and tell me once again what knowledge is. *B*

Theae: To say it's all opinion, Socrates, is out of one's power, since there's also false opinion, but there is a chance that true opinion is knowledge, and let that be my answer. For if it shows to us as we go on that it's not, we'll try to say something else, just as we're doing now.

Soc: This is surely the way one ought to speak, Theaetetus, eagerly rather than in the way you were shrinking from answering at first. For if we act in this way, one of two things will happen; either we'll discover the thing we're advancing on, or we'll be less apt to suppose we know what we don't know at all, and even that sort of reward is nothing to complain about. But now in particular, what exactly are you claiming? Since there is a pair of forms of opinion, one truthful and the other false, do you define knowledge as true opinion? *C*

Theae: I do, for this in turn now appears so to me.

Soc: Well, is it still worth it where opinion is concerned to take back up again—

Theae: What sort of thing are you talking about?

Soc: It troubles me somehow now, and often has at other times, so that I've come to be at a great loss with myself and with anyone else, that I don't have it in me to say *D* what in the world this experience is that's here with us, or in what way it comes to be present in us.

Theae: Of what sort, exactly?

Soc: That anyone has false opinions. So I'm considering it and now I'm still divided about whether we should let it go, or examine it carefully in a different way than we did a little before.[44]

Theae: What else, Socrates, if indeed it appears to be needed, even in any respect whatever? For just now you and Theodorus were talking about leisure, not badly at all, saying that there's no hurry in things of this sort.

E   **Soc:** You're correct in reminding me, since perhaps it's not a bad time to go back over our tracks, so to speak. For presumably its better to finish a little bit well than a lot inadequately.

Theae: What else?

Soc: How is it then? What exactly are we saying? Are we claiming that on every occasion when a false opinion is present, and some one of us has false opinions, someone else in turn has true ones, as though they were that way by nature?

Theae: That's exactly what we claim.

188A   **Soc:** Then accordingly, this is what's possible as far as we're concerned, in connection with all things and with them each by each, either to know or not to know? For learning and forgetting, as being between these, I say goodbye to in the present situation, since now, as far as we're concerned, they are nothing according to our statement.[45]

---

44   In 170C, the existence of false opinion was demonstrated by the fact that people in general believe in it, while Protagoras's principle prevents him from disagreeing with anyone's belief. What remains from that examination is a popular opinion, the inability of one school of thought to refute it, and our own unexamined experience.

45   Since learning was very much to the point in 186C, it must be the topic of opinion that has made it drop out of consideration. If opinion can only be true or false, and not on the way toward one or the other, and knowledge is placed within the class of opinion, then knowledge can only be wholly present or wholly absent.

Theae: But certainly, Socrates, there's nothing left about each thing except to know it or not know it.

Soc: Then it's necessary already that the one who has an opinion has it either about one of the things he knows or one he doesn't know?

Theae: It's necessary.

Soc: And surely, for the one who knows something not to know that very thing, or for the one who does not know it to know it, is out of one's power?

B

Theae: How could that not be so?

Soc: Then does the one who has false opinions suppose that the things he knows are not those things but some other things that he knows, so that knowing both, he's ignorant of both?

Theae: But that's out of one's power, Socrates.

Soc: Well then, does he consider things that he doesn't know to be some other things among those he doesn't know, so that it's possible for someone who knows neither Theaetetus nor Socrates to get it into his thinking that Socrates is Theaetetus or Theaetetus is Socrates?

Theae: How could that be?

C

Soc: But it's surely not that someone supposes things he knows to be things he doesn't know, or in turn that what he doesn't know is what he knows?

Theae: That would be a monstrosity.

Soc: How then is he still going to have false opinions? For outside these cases, there's presumably no power to have opinions, seeing as how for everything, we either know it or don't know it, and in these cases it appears there's nowhere that it's in one's power to have false opinions.

Theae: That's most true.

Soc: Well then, is what we're looking for something one ought not to examine in this way, going by one's knowing or not knowing, but rather by something's being or not?

D

Theae: How do you mean?

Soc: Maybe it's something simple, namely that there is no way that someone whose opinions about anything are of things that are not is not going to have false opinions, whatever the condition of his thinking may be in other respects.

Theae: That's more likely, Socrates.

Soc: How is it then? What will we say, Theaetetus, if someone cross-examines us: "And is what's being said in the power of anyone at all, and is any human being going to have as an opinion something that is not, whether it's about any of the beings or whether it's something itself by itself?" It seems likely we'd say, in response to these things, "Yes, whenever he's supposing and doesn't suppose true things." Or how will we answer?

E

Theae: That way.

Soc: And is there any such thing anywhere else?

Theae: What sort of thing?

Soc: If someone sees something, but sees nothing.

Theae: How could he?

Soc: But surely if he sees at least any one thing, he sees one of the beings; or do you suppose that what's one is ever among things that are not?

Theae: Not I.

Soc: Therefore, someone who sees at least any one thing sees something that *is*.

Theae: So it appears.

189A

Soc: And therefore, someone who hears anything hears some one thing at least, and hears something that *is*.

Theae: Yes.

Soc: And so does someone who touches any one thing at least also touch something that *is*, if indeed it's one?

Theae: That too.

Soc: So doesn't someone who has an opinion have an opinion about at least some one thing?

Theae: Necessarily.

Soc: And does someone who has an opinion about some one thing not have an opinion about something that *is*?

Theae: I go along with that.

Soc: Therefore, someone who has an opinion about something that *is not* has an opinion about nothing.

Theae: It appears not.

Soc: But surely someone who has an opinion about nothing doesn't even have an opinion at all.

Theae: That's clear, it seems.

Soc: Therefore it's not possible to have an opinion about something that *is not*, either in connection with the beings or itself by itself.

B

Theae: It appears not.

Soc: Therefore, having false opinions is something different from having opinions about things that *are not*.

Theae: It seems it's different.

Soc: Therefore, neither in this way nor in the way we were considering a little before, is there false opinion in us.

Theae: No, there certainly isn't.

Soc: Well then, do we give that name to something that happens in this way?

Theae: How?

Soc: We say that it's false opinion when there's a certain kind of otherwise-opinion, whenever someone, having made an exchange in his thinking, says that one of the beings is another of the beings in turn. For in this way he always has an opinion about something that *is*, but one thing in place of a different one, and by missing the target he was aiming at, he could justly be described as having false opinions.

C

Theae: You seem to me now to have said what's most correct. For whenever someone has an opinion with ugly in place of beautiful, or beautiful in place of ugly, then he truly has false opinions.

Soc: Obviously, Theaetetus, you are contemptuous of me and not afraid.

Theae: What are you talking about?

D

Soc: I suppose it didn't seem to you that I'd catch you up on your "truly false" by asking whether it's possible to become slowly quick or heavily light or for any other opposite thing to come to be opposite to itself in accord not with its own nature but with that of its opposite. Now I'll let that go, so that your confidence might not be frustrated; but you're satisfied, as you claim, that having false opinions is having otherwise-opinions?

Theae: I am.

Soc: Therefore, in your opinion, it's possible to set down one thing as another in one's thinking, and not as that thing.

Theae: Surely it's possible.

E

Soc: Then whenever anyone's thinking does this, isn't it also necessary that it be thinking either of both of them or of the one that's different?

Theae: Necessary indeed, at any rate either together or in turn.

Soc: Most beautiful. But is what you're calling thinking the same thing I am?

Theae: What is it you're calling that?

190A

Soc: Speech that the soul itself goes through with itself about whatever it considers. Of course it's as one who doesn't know that I'm declaring it to you. For it has this look to me, that when it's thinking the soul is doing nothing other than conversing, asking itself questions and answering them itself, and affirming and denying. But whenever it has made a determination, whether more slowly or with a quicker leap, and it asserts the same thing from that point on and is not divided, we set that down as its opinion. So I at least call forming opinion talking, and opinion a statement that's been made, though not to anyone else or with sound, but in silence to oneself. What about you?

Theae: I too.

Soc: Therefore, whenever anyone has the opinion that one thing is another, he also asserts to himself, as it seems, that the one thing is the other.

Theae: What else?   B

Soc: Then recollect whether you ever said to yourself that what's beautiful is more ugly than anything, or what's unjust is just. Or even the culmination of the whole thing: consider whether you ever tried to persuade yourself that one thing is, more than anything, some other thing, or whether it's entirely the opposite and not even in sleep did you ever dare to say to yourself that what's odd is absolutely even, or anything else of the sort.

Theae: What you say is true.

Soc: And do you suppose that anyone else, healthy or   C
insane, would dare to speak to himself in earnest, persuading himself that it's necessary for the cow to be a horse or for two to be one?

Theae: By Zeus, not I.

Soc: Then if forming an opinion is speaking to oneself, no one in speaking or forming an opinion about both of two things, and touching on them both with his soul, could say and have the opinion that one thing is another. Of course you have to disregard that sort of wording[46] in the case of what's other; I mean it this   D
way, that no one has the opinion that what's beautiful is ugly or anything else of that sort.

Theae: But I am disregarding it, Socrates, and it seems to me to be as you say.

---

46   In Greek, "one thing is another" is literally "another is another."

Soc: Therefore, in having an opinion about both of two things, it's out of one's power to have the opinion that one thing is another.

Theae: So it seems.

Soc: But surely in having an opinion that's about only one of them, and not at all about the other one, one will never have the opinion that one thing is another.

Theae: What you say is true, since it would be necessary for him also to be touching on the one his opinion is not about.

Soc: Therefore there's no room for anyone who has an opinion either about both of two things or about one of them to be having otherwise-opinion. And so, if anyone is going to define false opinion as having crosswise-opinion, it wouldn't have any meaning, for it's apparent that neither in this way nor by the previous ones is there false opinion in us.

E

Theae: It seems not.

Soc: But surely, Theaetetus, if that's not going to show up as being in us, we'll also be forced to agree to many unsettling things.

Theae: What sort of things?

Soc: I'm not going to tell you until I've tried to examine it in every way, since I'd be ashamed for us to be forced, in the place we've gotten lost in, to agree to the sort of things I'm referring to. But if we find our way and get free, then at that time we'll speak about them as things that other people are afflicted with, while we stand outside the ridicule; while if we're going to be at a loss in every way, then once we've been humiliated, I suppose we'll give up as though we were seasick for the argument to walk all over us and treat us however it wants. So listen to the way in which I still find a passageway for our inquiry.

191A

Theae: Just tell it.

Soc: I'll deny that we were correct to agree, at the point when we agreed it's out of one's power for one to

have the opinion that things he knows are things he
doesn't know, and get them false; but in a way it is in
his power.   *B*

Theae: Do you mean what I too suspected at the time when
we claimed it was that way, that sometimes, even
though I'm familiar with Socrates, when I see someone
else from far away that I'm not familiar with, I might
suppose him to be Socrates whom I know? For in such
a situation exactly the sort of thing you're talking
about happens.

Soc: But didn't we put that aside because what we know
would be making us not know, while we were
knowing?

Theae: Very much so.

Soc: So let's not put it that way, but in the following way;
· perhaps in some way it will be agreeable to us,   *C*
but perhaps it will strain our belief. But we've got
ourselves into the sort of fix in which it's necessary to
twist the argument around in every way in order to
test it. So consider whether I'm making any sense: is
it possible for someone who didn't know something
earlier to understand it later?

Theae: Of course it is.

Soc: And then in turn another thing and another?

Theae: How could it not be?

Soc: Then grant me for the sake of argument that there is
present in our souls a blob of wax, bigger in one person
and smaller in another, made of purer wax in one and
more filthy in another, and harder in some people but   *D*
more flexible in others, while there are some in whom
it's in a measured condition.

Theae: I grant it.

Soc: Then let's claim that it's a gift from Memory, mother of
the Muses, and that, whatever we want to remember
of the things we see or hear or think to ourselves, we
press into this by holding it under the perceptions and
thoughts, just as we make seals with the designs on

rings; and whatever gets molded, we remember and know for as long as the image of it is present, but whatever gets wiped out or becomes impossible to mold, we forget and do not know.

E

Theae: Let it be so.

Soc: Then consider whether in this way someone who knows them and is examining any of the things he sees or hears, might therefore have false opinions.

Theae: In what sort of way?

Soc: By sometimes supposing the things he knows to be the things he knows, but sometimes things he doesn't know. For in what went before, the way we agreed about these things, when we agreed they were out of one's power, was not so beautiful.

Theae: What do you say about them now?

192A

Soc: They need to be spoken about from the beginning with distinctions made in the following way: whatever someone knows, when one has a memorial of it in his soul but isn't perceiving it, it's out of one's power to suppose is some other thing he knows, having also an impress of that but not perceiving it; and again it's out of one's power to suppose that a thing he knows is a thing he doesn't know and doesn't have a seal of, and that a thing he doesn't know is another thing he doesn't know, and that a thing he doesn't know is a thing he knows; and to suppose that a thing he's perceiving is some other thing he's perceiving, and that a thing he's perceiving is one of the things he's not perceiving, and

B

that a thing he's not perceiving is one of things he's not perceiving, and that a thing he's not perceiving is one of the things he's perceiving; and yet again to suppose that a thing he knows and is perceiving and is holding its imprint against the perception, is any other of the things he knows and is perceiving and is also holding the imprint of that against the perception, is still more out of one's power than the former cases, if that's possible, and it's out of one's power to suppose that a thing he knows and is perceiving, holding it to its memorial correctly, is a thing he knows, and that a

thing he knows and is perceiving, holding it under the   C
same conditions, is a thing he's perceiving; and again
that a thing he doesn't know and isn't perceiving is a
thing that he doesn't know and isn't perceiving, and
that a thing he doesn't know and isn't perceiving
is a thing he doesn't know, and that a thing he
doesn't know and isn't perceiving is a thing he's not
perceiving. For all these cases, it goes beyond anything
in powerlessness to have any false opinion in them. So
it remains in the following cases, if anywhere else, for
such a thing to happen.

Theae: In what cases exactly? If even then I'm going to
understand anything more from them, since I'm not
following now.

Soc: In the case of things that one knows, for him to suppose
them to be some other things that he knows and
is perceiving; or that they're things that he doesn't
know but is perceiving; or that things he knows   D
and is perceiving are other things he knows and is
perceiving.[47]

Theae: Now I'm left behind much more than I was then.

Soc: Then listen to them back over again in this way: if I
know Theodorus and remember in myself what he's
like, and Theaetetus in the same manner, isn't it still
the case that sometimes I see them and sometimes not,
and at one time I touch them but at another I don't,
and I hear them or perceive them with some other
sense, but at another time I have no perception at all of
you, but nonetheless I remember you and I myself, in
myself, know you?

Theae: Very much so.   E

Soc: Then understand that this is the first of the things I
want to show, that it is possible not to perceive the
things one knows, and it is possible to perceive them.

Theae: That's true.

---

47   This array of instances lacks clarity though it has great precision. The reader who
keeps track of the cases will discover that seventeen of them are given, which
recalls the series of demonstrations Theodorus had constructed (147D).

Soc: Then too with the things one doesn't know, is it possible on many occasions not to perceive them either, and on many occasions to perceive them only?

Theae: That's possible too.

193A

Soc: Then see whether you can fix your attention on it any better now. If Socrates is familiar with Theodorus and Theaetetus, but sees neither of them, and no other perception about them is present to him either, he could not at that time have in himself the opinion that Theaetetus is Theodorus. Am I making some sense or none at all?

Theae: Yes, and it's true.

Soc: This, then, was the first of the cases I was describing.

Theae: Yes it was.

Soc: Then the second case is that, being familiar with one of you but not being familiar with the other, and perceiving neither of you, again at that time I could not suppose the one I know to be the one I don't know.

Theae: Correct.

B

Soc: And the third is, being familiar with neither of you and not perceiving either of you, I could not suppose someone I don't know to be some other person I don't know. And consider that you've heard all the other cases from before again in order, in which I'll never have false opinions about you and Theodorus, whether I'm familiar with or ignorant of both, or familiar with one but not the other; and in the cases of perceptions in the same ways, if you follow by inference.

Theae: I do follow.

C

Soc: Then it remains to have false opinions in this situation, whenever, being familiar with you and Theodorus, and having the imprints of the pair of you in that piece of wax as if from signet rings, seeing you both from a long way and not adequately, I'm eager to assign the particular imprint of each one to the sight that belongs to it, making it step into and fit its own footprint in order for recognition[48] to come about, and then getting them mixed up, like people who put their shoes on the wrong feet, I interchange them and slap the sight of each one on the imprint that belongs to the other, or even the sorts of things that happen to sight in mirrors, when things on the right flow across to the left, when the same thing happens to me I make a mistake. So it's then that crosswise-opinion and having a false opinion result.   **D**

Theae: It does seem likely, Socrates. How wonderfully you describe the experience of opinion.

Soc: Then there's still also what happens whenever, being familiar with both, I perceive one in addition to being familiar with him, and not the other, but I don't hold the familiarity with the former against the perception, which is the way I described it in what went before, and then you didn't understand me.

Theae: No, I didn't.

Soc: I meant this, that being familiar with the one and perceiving him, and holding the familiarity against the perception, one will never suppose him to be anyone else whom he's familiar with and perceives and also holds his familiarity with that one against the perception. Was that it?   **E**

Theae: Yes.

Soc: But the case that was being described just now was apparently left out, namely that in which we claim false opinion comes about when someone who's familiar with both and seeing both, or having some other perception of the pair of them, holds the pair of imprints not each against its own perception, but just as a low-grade bowman shoots an arrow, he swerves past the target and misses his mark, which, therefore, is exactly what is called false.   **194A**

---

48   This reminds one of Electra's recognition of her brother's presence in Aeschylus's *Libation Bearers*, 205-210, but that example casts doubt on the whole wax analogy, since the brother and sister have identical footprints. Even in the fourteen cases where error was supposed to be impossible, a third person could get them confused without making any mistakes.

Theae: In all likelihood, anyway.

Soc: And then whenever a perception is present for one of the imprints, but not for the other, and one's thinking fits the imprint of the absent perception up against the one that's present, in every instance of this the thinking is false. And in one sentence, about things one doesn't *B* know and never perceived, there is, as it seems, no being wrong and no false opinion, if anything we're saying now is sound, but about things we do know and are perceiving, it's just in these that opinion twists and turns, becoming false and true, true when it brings together its impressions with their own imprints directly opposite and turned straight, but false when they're off to the sides and twisted.

Theae: Well isn't that beautifully put, Socrates?

C **Soc:** You'll say it still more once you've heard the following things. For having true opinions is a beautiful thing, and being wrong is an ugly thing.

Theae: How could it be otherwise?

Soc: Well, they say these things come about from this: whenever the wax in someone's soul is deep, plentiful, smooth, and softened up in a measured way, the things that come through the perceptions, pressing their seals into this "heart" of the soul, as Homer calls it, making a cryptic allusion to wax,[49] then and in these people *D* the imprints that come to be present are pure and have sufficient depth to be long lasting, and such people are quick to learn in the first place, and then are good at remembering, so that they don't get the imprints of their perceptions mixed up, but do have true opinions. For since the molds are distinct and in a roomy place, these people quickly sort out, each into its own mold, the things that are called beings, and so it's they who are called wise.[50] Or doesn't it seem that way to you?

---

49   The older and poetic variant of the word for heart sounded like the word for wax. This is a bit like saying "Shakespeare used the word 'hark' as a cryptic allusion to the ark."

50   This passage might be compared with *Republic* VII, 516C-D.

Theae: Supernaturally so.

Soc: Then whenever anyone's heart is shaggy, which the   *E*
poet wise in all things approves of,[51] or whenever
it's mucked up and not made of pure wax, or it's too
fluid or too hard, those in whom it's fluid are quick
to learn but become forgetful, and those in whom it's
hard are the opposite. But the ones who have a shaggy
and rough heart that's in any way gravelly, filled
with dirt or manure that's mixed into it, have their
molds indistinct, as those with hard hearts also have
indistinct molds, since there's no depth in them. And
they're indistinct as well for those with fluid hearts,   *195A*
since they become blurred as a result of running
together quickly. And if, in addition to all these
things, they've landed on top of one another from a
lack of room, in case someone has a little mini-soul,
they're still more indistinct than those. All these, then,
become the sort of people who have false opinions,
for whenever they see or hear or think of anything,
since they don't have the power to sort each of them
out quickly to each mold, they're slow, and by sorting
things into the wrong places they mis-see and mishear
and mistake most things in their thinking, and these in
turn are said to be in the wrong about the beings and
to be without understanding.

Theae: These are the most correct things human beings   *B*
could say, Socrates.

Soc: Therefore we assert that there are false opinions in us?

Theae: Vehemently.

Soc: And true ones?

Theae: True ones too.

---

51   The joke here consists of mocking a figure of speech by taking it literally. At I,
189, of the *Iliad*, Homer refers to the heart in Achilles' hairy (or shaggy) chest,
and then at II, 851 and XVI, 554, he applies the adjective directly to the hearts
of two other characters; the lines are effective, merging the image of a rough
exterior with the suggestion of a tough fighting spirit (or heart). The butt of the
joke is not the poet, or people who quote him, but the attempt to explain thinking
as something bodily.

Soc: Then do we suppose that at this point we've come to sufficient agreement that, more certainly than anything, this pairing of opinions is present both together?

Theae: Supernaturally so.

Soc: How true it runs the risk of being, Theaetetus, that a long-winded man is a terrible and unpleasant thing.

Theae: What? What prompted you to say that?

C   **Soc:** Being disgusted at my own thickheadedness and true long-windedness. For what other name could anyone give it when someone pulls his words upside down because, from stupidity, he's powerless to be convinced, and hard to pry loose from each thing he says?[52]

Theae: But why are *you* disgusted?

Soc: I'm not only disgusted but even afraid about what I'd answer if someone asked me: "Well, Socrates, have you discovered that false opinion is neither in perceptions in relation to one another nor in thoughts, D   but in the connection of perception with thinking?" I'll acknowledge it, I suppose, with a simpering expression on my face, as though we had discovered something beautiful.

Theae: Well to me at least, Socrates, there doesn't seem to be anything ugly about the thing that's now been demonstrated.

Soc: "So then," he says, "you're saying that we'd never suppose the human being we only think about, but don't see, to be a horse, which in turn we don't see or touch, but only think about and don't perceive anything about?" I suppose I'll acknowledge that I am saying that.

---

52 The parade of words with the prefix mis- (*para-*) at the end of 195A is replaced here with a similar parade of the prefix *dus-*. (The best imitation of that effect the translator could think of was "learning disability" for "thickheadedness" and "disinclined to disconnect" for "hard to pry loose.") The identification of knowledge with true opinion puts knowledge and error on the same level, and makes error a (mis)taking of one thing for another; this retraction of one version of it points to a deeper understanding of error as rooted in a dis-abling lack of a power or potency.

Theae: And correctly too.

Soc: "Well then," he says, "what about the eleven that one   *E*
does nothing other than think; does this argument say
otherwise than that one could never suppose it to be
twelve that one also only thinks?" Come on then; you
answer.

Theae: And I'll answer that someone seeing or touching
eleven things might suppose the eleven to be twelve,
but he could never have that opinion about the eleven
itself that he's holding in his thinking.

Soc: What about this? Do you suppose anyone ever set before
himself, in himself, for examination, five and seven,   *196A*
and I don't mean seven and five people or anything
else of that sort, but five and seven themselves, which
we're claiming are there as imprints in the blob of wax,
and that among them there can't be any false opinions,
in regard to these themselves did any human being
ever yet examine them, talking to himself and asking
how many they are, and one person said, believing it,
that they are eleven, while another said twelve, or does
everyone say and believe them to be twelve?

Theae: No, by Zeus, but many do say eleven, and in fact if   *B*
one looks into a larger number, there's more tripping
up; for I suppose you're talking about every number.

Soc: You suppose correctly. And take this to heart: is
anything else then happening than that one is
supposing the twelve itself that's in the blob of wax to
be eleven?

Theae: That seems likely, at any rate.

Soc: Then hasn't that come back again to the first things that
were said? For the one who experiences this supposes,
about a thing he knows, that it's a different one of the
things that he also knows, which we claimed is out of
one's power, and it's by that very means that we forced
there to be no false opinion, so that the same person   *C*
wouldn't be forced not to know the same things at the
same time he knew them.

Theae: Most true.

Soc: But then one has to show that having false opinions is anything but the swerving of a thought in relation to a perception, for if it were that, we could never be wrong in the thoughts themselves. But now, you see, either there is no false opinion, or it's possible not to know the things one knows. And of these, which do you choose?

Theae: You're putting forward a choice there's no way through, Socrates.

D   **Soc:** But surely there's no chance that the argument is going to allow them both. Nevertheless—since one ought to be brave enough for any risk—what if we were to try to do something shameless?

Theae: In what way?

Soc: By being willing to say what sort of thing knowing is.

Theae: And why is that a shameless thing?

Soc: You don't seem to grasp that the whole discussion of ours from the start has been a search for knowledge on the assumption that we don't know what it is.

Theae: I grasp that.

Soc: Then doesn't it seem shameless for people who don't know knowledge to declare what sort of thing knowing
E   is? But really, Theaetetus, we've been infected for a long time with impure talk. For tens of thousands of times we've said "we recognize" and "we don't recognize," and "we know" and "we don't know," as though we understand one another in some way while still being ignorant of knowledge; and, if you please, even now at present we've again used "being ignorant" and "understand," as though it's appropriate to use them if we're doing without knowledge.

Theae: But in what way will you have a conversation, Socrates, if you abstain from these words?

197A   **Soc:** In no way, since I am who I am, though I would if I were someone who makes a practice of contradicting;

if such a man were present even now, he'd tell us to abstain from them and throw what I'm saying vehemently back in our teeth. Since we're just lowly folks, do you want me to have the daring to say what sort of thing knowing is? For it appears to me that something productive would come of it.

Theae: Dare it then, by Zeus. And there'll be plenty of forgiveness for your not abstaining from these words.

Soc: Have you heard, then, what people now say knowing is?

Theae: Possibly, but I'm not remembering at present.

Soc: Surely people claim it's a having of knowledge.   *B*

Theae: True.

Soc: We, then, might change it a little and say it's a possessing of knowledge.

Theae: And in what way exactly will you claim the latter differs from the former?

Soc: Perhaps in none, but when you've heard how it seems to, test it out with me.

Theae: If I'm able to, at any rate.

Soc: Now having doesn't appear to me to be the same thing as possessing. For instance, if someone has bought a cloak and is in control of it, but isn't wearing it, we wouldn't claim that he had it, but certainly that he possessed it.

Theae: And correctly.

Soc: Then see if it's also in one's power to possess   *C*
knowledge in that way without having it, but just as if someone who was hunting wild birds, pigeons or any other kind, having set up a pigeon coop at home, were to raise them there, we'd presumably claim that in a certain way he always has them, because he possesses them, wouldn't we?

Theae: Yes.

Soc: But in another way he doesn't have a single one, but a power over them has come to be at his disposal, since he brought them under his hand in a private enclosure, to grab and hold whenever he wants, once he's hunted down whichever one he wishes at any time, and to let them go again, and he has the power to do this as many times as he sees fit.

D

Theae: These things are so.

Soc: So again, just as in the preceding discussion we made up some sort of wax contrivance in our souls—I don't know what—now again let's make some sort of pigeon coop in each soul for all sorts of birds, some in flocks apart from the rest, others in small bunches, and some alone, flying through them all however they happen to.

E

Theae: Let it have been made. But what's the upshot of it?

Soc: One ought to claim that when we're children this container is empty, and to think of pieces of knowledge instead of birds; and whatever piece of knowledge anyone confines in this enclosure when he's acquired it, one ought to say he's learned or discovered the thing this was the knowledge of, and that this is knowing.[53]

Theae: Let it be so.

198A

Soc: Then as for hunting down again whichever piece of knowledge one wants, and holding it when one has grabbed it, and letting it go again, consider what names are needed, whether they're the same as when one first acquired them or different. And you'll understand what I mean more clearly from this: you speak of an art of arithmetic?

Theae: Yes.

Soc: Then conceive of that as a hunting for pieces of knowledge about everything that's even or odd.

Theae: I'm conceiving that.

---

53 Consistently through the discussion of opinion, Socrates pictures it as the inert, passive, or unattended-to residue of some previous activity. Consider 190A and 191D. The active having and holding that has just been mentioned would be something other than having an opinion.

Soc: Now it's by this art, I suppose, that he keeps at hand
the pieces of knowledge about numbers and also by it
that one who hands them over to someone else hands
them over.

B

Theae: Yes.

Soc: And we speak of the one who hands them over as
teaching and the one who takes them to himself as
learning, and hence of the one who has them, by
possessing them in that pigeon coop, as knowing.

Theae: Entirely so.

Soc: Now turn your attention to what follows directly
from this. When someone is completely skilled at
arithmetic, does that mean anything else than that he
knows all numbers? For the pieces of knowledge about
all numbers belong to him in his soul.

Theae: What else?

Soc: Then would such a person ever count anything, either
himself by himself counting the numbers themselves,
or counting anything else among those external things
that have a number?

C

Theae: How could it be otherwise?

Soc: And we'll set it down that the counting is nothing other
than examining how big any number happens to be.

Theae: That's so.

Soc: Therefore, the one whom we've agreed knows all
number, when he's examining, shows himself as not
knowing the thing he knows. You presumably hear
about disputes of that sort.

Theae: I do.

Soc: Then since we're making an image of the possession
and hunting of pigeons, we'll say that the hunting
was two-fold, one of them before acquiring, for the
sake of possessing, the other by the possessor for the
sake of grabbing and holding in his hands what he has
possessed for some time. So too, about those things
of which there were pieces of knowledge belonging

D

for some time to someone who has learned them and has known them, there is such a thing as thoroughly understanding these same things again by taking back up and holding the knowledge of each thing that he'd possessed for some time, but didn't have at hand in his thinking?

Theae: That's true.

E

Soc: This is exactly what I was asking just now: how ought one to use the names to speak about them when someone skilled at arithmetic enters upon counting or a literate person enters upon reading, since, therefore, in such a case, though he knows, he's going back for the purpose of learning from himself what he knows?

Theae: But that's unsettling, Socrates.

199A

Soc: But are we to say he's going to read or to count things that he doesn't know, though we've granted to him that he knows all letters, or all number?

Theae: But that's senseless too.

Soc: Then do you want us to say that none of the names is of any concern to us, in whichever way anyone enjoys dragging around "knowing" and "learning," but since we've determined that it's one thing to possess knowledge but another thing to have it, we claim that it's impossible for someone not to possess what he's acquired, so that no one ever turns out not to know what he knows, though it is possible to take up a false opinion about it? For it is possible not to have the knowledge of it, but some other in its place, whenever in hunting for some piece of knowledge somewhere at some time, while they're fluttering around, mistaking it, he takes up one in place of another; therefore at such a time, he supposes twelve to be eleven, taking up the knowledge of eleven that's in himself in place of that of twelve, as if it were a ring-necked dove instead of a pigeon.

B

Theae: Now that has sense in it.

Soc: Then whenever one takes up what he puts his hand out to take up, at such a time he is without falsity and has

the things that are as opinions, and so in this way there
is both true and false opinion, and none of the things
we were inconvenienced by in the previous discussion
becomes an obstacle? Perhaps then you'll give me your
agreement; or what will you do?

C

Theae: That.

Soc: In fact we've gotten rid of the not knowing the things
people know, since it no longer turns out anywhere
that we don't possess what we possess, either when
we're wrong about anything or when we're not.
However, another misfortune, a more terrible one,
seems to me to be revealing itself.

Theae: Of what sort?

Soc: If the interchange of pieces of knowledge is ever going
to become a false opinion.

Theae: How's that?

Soc: In the first place, for someone who has knowledge of
anything to be ignorant of that very thing, not by means
of ignorance but by means of his own knowledge, and
next, to have the opinion that this is something else and
something else in turn is this, how is that not a load
of nonsense, when, with knowledge present, the soul
recognizes nothing and is ignorant of everything? On
the basis of this account, nothing prevents ignorance,
when it's present, from making one know something, or
blindness from making one see, if indeed knowledge is
ever going to make someone be ignorant of anything.

D

Theae: Then perhaps, Socrates, we didn't set up the birds in
a beautiful way when we only set them down as pieces
of knowledge, and it was necessary also to put in
pieces of nonknowledge flying around together with
them in the soul, and for the hunter sometimes to take
hold of a piece of knowledge and sometimes of a piece
of nonknowledge about the same thing, having a false
opinion with the nonknowledge and a true one with
the knowledge.

E

Soc: It's not easy, Theaetetus, not to praise you; however,
take a good look again at what you're saying. For let

200A   it be as you say; the one who takes hold of a piece of nonknowledge will, you claim, have a false opinion, won't he?

Theae: Yes.

Soc: But presumably he's not going to think he has a false opinion.

Theae: How could he?

Soc: But a true one, and his attitude will be that of someone who knows the things about which he's wrong.

Theae: What else?

Soc: Therefore he'll suppose he has knowledge, when he's hunted for it, and not nonknowledge.

Theae: That's clear.

Soc: Then after we've gone a long way around, we are back at our first impasse. For that skilled refuter will
B   laugh and say, "Best of fellows, will someone who knows both a piece of knowledge and a piece of nonknowledge suppose that one of them, which he knows, is some other thing that he knows; or knowing neither of them, does he have the opinion that what he doesn't know is something else that he doesn't know; or knowing one of them but not the other will he think what he knows is what he doesn't know or what he doesn't know is what he knows? Or will you tell me next that there are also pieces of knowledge about the pieces of knowledge and nonknowledge, which the one possessing them has enclosed in some
C   other ridiculous pigeon coops or wax contrivances, and knows for as long as he possesses them, even if he doesn't have them at hand in his soul? And in that way will you force yourselves to run back around to the same place thousands of times, making no headway?" What will we answer to these things, Theaetetus?

Theae: By Zeus, Socrates, I don't have any idea what one ought to say.

Soc: Then, my boy, doesn't the argument give us a beautiful rebuke, and point out that it was not correct for us to

look for false opinion before knowledge, leaving that **D**
alone? But the former is something one has no power
to recognize before one gets a sufficient grasp of what
knowledge is.

Theae: It's necessary, Socrates, in the present circumstances
to suppose it to be as you say.

Soc: What then will anyone say knowledge is, back again
from the start? For surely we're not going to give it up
yet?

Theae: Not in the least; that is, unless you renounce it.

Soc: Speak up then; what's the most we can say about it that
would put us least in opposition to our own selves?

Theae: Just the thing we were trying out in what went **E**
before, Socrates; since I at least have nothing else.

Soc: What sort of thing?

Theae: That true opinion is knowledge. Having a true opinion
is surely something safe from error at least, and all the
things that come from it are beautiful and good.

Soc: That will show up directly, Theaetetus, as the river
guide said; and if we examine that, then perhaps as we
go along the very thing we're seeking might make an *201A*
appearance, and turn out to be at our feet, but nothing
will be clear to us if we stand still.

Theae: What you say is correct; so let's go on and examine it.

Soc: Well this is a matter for a short examination anyway,
since a whole art indicates that it isn't knowledge.

Theae: How's that? And which art is this?

Soc: The one that belongs to those who are the greatest for
wisdom, who are called rhetoricians and lawyers, since
these people by their own art surely persuade without
teaching, and make someone have whatever opinion
they want. Or do you suppose that any teachers are so
terrifyingly skilled that they have the power, during **B**
the flow of a little water,[54] to teach anyone adequately

---

54   See the note to 172E.

the truth about what happened to some people, with whom they themselves were not present, who were robbed of money or suffered some other violence?

Theae: I don't suppose that at all, but only to persuade them.

Soc: And by persuading, don't you mean making them have an opinion?

Theae: What else?

C

Soc: Then whenever the jurors are justly persuaded about things it's possible to know only by seeing them and in no other way, at a time when they're deciding these things from hearing about them and getting hold of a true opinion, haven't they decided without knowledge, even though, if they judged well, they were persuaded of correct things?[55]

Theae: Absolutely.

Soc: Then, dear fellow, if true opinion and knowledge were the same thing in a courtroom, a top-notch juror never could have had correct opinions without knowledge, but as things are, they seem to be each something different.

D

Theae: That's what I heard someone saying, Socrates, but forgot, but now it comes to me. He said that true opinion with an articulation is knowledge, but one that lacks an articulation is beyond knowledge; and those things of which there is no articulation are not intelligible—he used just that name—but those that have one are intelligible.[56]

---

55 There is now a linkage of opinion, correctness, and hearing on one side, as opposed to knowledge, truth, and seeing or touching on the other.

56 Two words in this speech need comments. The word translated "intelligible" could be straightforwardly translated as "knowable," but that would lose the flavor of something novel or unusual that Theaetetus remarks on; a different word was commonly used to mean knowable, and Socrates uses it below. The more important word is the one translated "articulation," which is *logos*. In its immediate context, it means something like "rational account" (and it is translated elsewhere in the dialogue as "statement," "argument," or "discussion"), but Socrates will open the word up to a much wider range of interpretations to explore what such an account might be. (See especially 206C-D, 206D-207A, and 208C.) Since this *logos* purports to be the thing that binds the perceptible and the intelligible, in the context of the dialogue as a whole, it amounts to some kind of return to the central question asked of Theaetetus in 187A.

Soc: What you say is surely beautiful, but say in what respect exactly he distinguished these intelligible and not-intelligible things, in case you and I have heard it the same way.

Theae: I don't know whether I'll dredge it up; however, as I suppose, if someone else were to say, I could follow it.

Soc: Then listen to a dream in return for a dream, since I in my turn seemed to hear from some people that the primary things, something very much like elements, out of which we and everything else are composed, could have no articulation. For each of them itself by itself could only be named, but it's out of one's power to apply any other description, not even that it *is* or isn't, since that would already be connecting being or not-being with it, while one must not attach anything to it if one is going to speak about that thing itself alone. One ought not even to attach "itself" or "that" or "each" or "alone" or "this," or many other such things, for these things run around and get attached to everything, though they're different from the things they're connected with; it ought, if it were possible for it to be spoken of and have its own proper articulation, to be spoken of without all these other things, but as it is, it's impossible for any whatever of the primary things to be stated in an articulation. There's nothing for it other than to be named only, since it has only a name, but the things made of these are already composite, and just as they are intertwined, so too when their names are intertwined in the same way there has come to be an articulation, since the very being of an articulation is an intertwining of names. So in that way the elements are inarticulable and unknowable, though they're perceptible, but the compounds are knowable and speakable and capable of being held in a true opinion. So whenever anyone gets hold of a true opinion without an articulation, his soul tells the truth about it without recognizing that, since anyone who doesn't have the power to give and accept an articulation is lacking knowledge about that thing, but once he also gets hold of an articulation, a power over all these things has come to him and

E

202A

B

C

a perfect condition has come to hold in him toward knowledge. Did you hear it that way in your dreams, or some other way?

Theae: That way absolutely.

Soc: Are you satisfied, then, to set it down this way too, that true opinion with an articulation is knowledge?

Theae: Precisely so.

D   **Soc:** Well, Theaetetus, have we really gotten hold in this way on this day of something that many wise men also sought after long ago and grew old before discovering?

Theae: It seems to me at any rate, Socrates, that what's now stated is beautifully articulated.

Soc: And it's likely, as far as it goes, that this very thing is so, for what knowledge could there still be in separation from an articulation and a correct opinion? One thing in what was stated, though, is dissatisfying to me.

Theae: What sort of thing exactly?

Soc: The one that seemed to be the most exquisitely
E   articulated, that the elements are unknowable, but the class of compounds is knowable.

Theae: Isn't it correct?

Soc: That's exactly what one needs to know; and we have, like hostages for the argument, the patterns he was using when he said all these things.

Theae: What sort of patterns?

Soc: The letters and syllables of written words.[57] Or do you suppose the person who said the things we're talking about was looking anywhere else when he said them?

Theae: No, at these.

---

57   The Greek words used for elements and compounds are the same words that mean letters and syllables.

Soc: Then by taking them back up again, or rather by taking ourselves back up again,[58] let's test whether we learned spelling that way or not. Well then, first, the syllables have an articulation but the letters are inarticulable?

Theae: Maybe.

Soc: Very much so, it appears to me. At any rate, if someone were to ask about the first syllable of Socrates in this way—"Theaetetus, tell me, what is SO?"—what will you answer?

Theae: That it's sigma and omega.

Soc: Then don't you have this articulation of the syllable?

Theae: I do.

Soc: Come on then and state in that way the articulation of sigma.

B

Theae: How is anyone going to state an element of the element? And in particular, Socrates, the sigma is one of the unvoiced ones, only a sound, as of the tongue hissing; and for beta, in turn, there's neither voice nor sound, nor is there for most of the letters. So it holds up quite well for them to be called inarticulable, when the most distinct of them are the very seven that have voice only, and no articulation whatever.[59]

Soc: Therefore on this point, my companion, we've got it correct about knowledge.

Theae: We appear to.

---

58 In 193 the appearance of the people present was the example used for forming opinions; here it will be their names that are articulated. One may recall that Theaetetus has Socrates's face and a young companion of his (147D), who is also present, has his name.

59 Theaetetus, as accurate a grammarian as he is a mathematician, is referring to the seven distinctly voiced vowels, produced by vibrating the vocal chords. Of the seventeen consonants, nine are mutes or stops that cannot even be pronounced in isolation from a vowel, since they are ways of stopping or shaping another sound with the lips (pi, beta, and phi), teeth (tau, delta, and theta), or palate (kappa, gamma, and chi); the sibilant sigma, the liquids lambda and rho, and the nasals mu and nu are sounded but not voiced, as are the three compound consonants zeta, ksi, and psi.

Soc: Then what? Have we correctly accepted the claim that the letter is not knowable but the syllable is?

Theae: It seems likely.

Soc: Come then; do we mean the syllable is both the letters together, or if there are more than two, all of them, or some one look that has come into being when they've been put together?

Theae: We seem to me to mean it's all of them.

Soc: So look at the two, sigma and omega; both together are the first syllable of my name. Does the one who recognizes it recognize anything other than both together?

D **Theae:** What else?

Soc: Therefore he recognizes the sigma and the omega.

Theae: Yes.

Soc: Then what? He's ignorant of each, and knowing neither one he recognizes both together?

Theae: But that's a terrible and unspeakable thing, Socrates.

Soc: But surely if it's necessary to recognize each of them, if indeed one is to recognize them both together, there's every necessity for the one who's ever going to recognize the syllable to have a prior recognition of all the letters, and so the beautiful account of ours will be swept off and run away.

E **Theae:** And very suddenly at that.

Soc: It's because we're not doing a beautiful job of watching over it. For perhaps one ought to have set down the syllable not as the letters but as some one form having come out of them, having itself its own single look, different from the letters.

Theae: Very much so, and it probably would be more the latter way than the former.

Soc: One ought to examine it and not desert in so unmanly a way a great and solemn account.

Theae: No indeed.

Soc: Then let it hold in the way we're now claiming, that **204A** the syllable is a single look that comes out of each and every letter when they're fitted together, in the case of letters of the alphabet and of all other things alike.

Theae: Very much so.

Soc: Then it must not have parts.

Theae: Why, exactly?

Soc: Because with a thing of which there are parts, it's necessary for the whole to be all the parts. Or do you say that the whole that has come into being out of the parts is also some one form, different from all the parts?

Theae: I do.

Soc: So do you speak of the all and the whole as the same thing, or of each of them as something different? **B**

Theae: I have nothing clear, but because you urge me to answer confidently, taking a bold risk, I say that they're different.

Soc: The confidence, Theaetetus, is correct, but whether the answer is too needs to be examined.

Theae: It certainly does need to.

Soc: Then the whole would be different from the all, according to the present account?

Theae: Yes.

Soc: And what about this? Is it possible that all the things are different from the all? For example, whenever we say one, two, three, four, five, six, if we also say two **C** times three or three times two or four plus two or three plus two plus one, in every one of these cases are we speaking of the same thing or of something different?

Theae: The same thing.

Soc: Is it anything other than six?

Theae: Nothing else.

Soc: Then in each way of saying it we've spoken of all six?

Theae: Yes.

Soc: But when we speak of them all are we not speaking of an all?

Theae: Necessarily.

Soc: Is it anything other than the six?

Theae: Nothing else.

D   **Soc:** Therefore it's the same one thing that we're addressing ourselves to as the all and all the things, at least for whatever is made of number?

Theae: It appears to be.

Soc: Then let's speak about them in the following way. The number of the plethron[60] and the plethron are the same thing, aren't they?

Theae: Yes.

Soc: And it's the same way with the number of the stade?

Theae: Yes.

Soc: And so also the number of the army and the army, and similarly with all such things? With each of them, all the number is all the thing.

Theae: Yes.

E   **Soc:** And the number belonging to each thing is nothing other than its parts?

Theae: Nothing else.

Soc: Then as many things as have parts would be made of parts?

Theae: It appears so.

Soc: But all the parts are then agreed to be the all, if indeed all the number is also going to be the all.

Theae: That's so.

---

60   As a unit of length, of 100 feet, the plethron is nothing but a numerical measure, and the Greek word *arithmos* applied just as much to any multitudes as to the pure numbers of arithmetic. But the next example, the stade, is not only 6 plethra, but the length of the race track at the Olympic games, and hence a standard word for a race course; it is not merely a quantitative aggregate.

Soc: Therefore the whole is not made of parts, since then it would be an all, being all the parts.

Theae: It seems not.

Soc: But is it possible that a part is the very thing that it is as belonging to anything else whatever than to the whole?

Theae: Well, to the all.

Soc: You're battling in a manly way, Theaetetus. But as for *205A* the all, whenever nothing is lacking, isn't that very thing all?

Theae: Necessarily.

Soc: And won't a whole be that same thing, from which nothing is missing in any way? But that from which something is missing is neither a whole nor an all, which have come to be the same thing, at the same time, made of the same thing?

Theae: It seems to me now that an all and a whole don't differ at all.

Soc: Then weren't we saying that whatever has parts, the thing that is whole and all, will be all its parts?

Theae: Exactly.

Soc: So once again there's the very thing I was making an attempt at just now: isn't it necessary that, if the *B* compound is not the elements, it doesn't have the elements as parts of itself, or if the compound is the same as the elements, it is knowable in the same way they are?

Theae: That's so.

Soc: And wasn't it in order for this not to happen that we set it down as different from them?

Theae: Yes.

Soc: Then what? If the elements are not parts of the compound, do you have any other things to mention that are parts of the compound but are not elements of it?

Theae: Not at all. For if I go along with saying there are any parts of it, it's surely ridiculous to send away the elements and go after something else.

C **Soc:** So it's absolutely the case, Theaetetus, according to our present discussion, that the compound would be a single indivisible look.

Theae: That seems likely.

Soc: Do you remember then, dear fellow, that a little while ago we accepted, considering that it was well said, that there could be no articulation of the primary things out of which everything else is composed, for the reason that each of them itself by itself would be without composition, and that it wouldn't be correct even to apply "to be" in speaking about it, or "this," on the grounds that one would be speaking of things different from it and foreign to it, and precisely this cause would make it inarticulable and unknowable?

Theae: I remember.

D **Soc:** Then is there any other cause than this of its being single in form and indivisible? I don't see any other.

Theae: It appears then that there isn't.

Soc: Then hasn't the compound fallen into the same form as the element, if indeed it doesn't have parts and is a single look?

Theae: Absolutely.

Soc: Therefore, if the compound is many elements and some sort of whole, and these elements are parts of it, then the compounds and the elements are alike knowable and speakable, since all the parts showed up as the same thing as the whole.

E **Theae:** Certainly.

Soc: But if it's one and without parts, then not only compound but element in the same way are alike inarticulable and unknowable, since the same cause will make them that way.

Theae: I don't have anything different to say.

Soc: Therefore, let's not accept this, no matter who says a compound is knowable and speakable and an element is the opposite.

Theae: Let's not; if, that is, we're persuaded by the argument.

Soc: What about this, in turn? If someone said the opposite, *206A* wouldn't you accept that instead, based on the inside knowledge you yourself have from yourself by learning the letters of the alphabet?

Theae: What sort?

Soc: That in learning them you persevered in nothing other than trying to distinguish each of the letters, itself by itself, by sight and by hearing, in order that their arrangement would not confuse you when they were spoken or written.

Theae: What you say is most true.

Soc: And at the harpist's place, would having learned perfectly be anything other than having the power to *B* follow each note—to what string it belongs—which everyone would agree are spoken of as the elements of music?

Theae: Nothing else.

Soc: Therefore in those things in which we ourselves are experienced with elements and compounds, if one ought to conclude from evidence from these things to everything else as well, we'll assert that the class of elements has a more distinct and more authoritative recognition than that of compounds, for getting hold of each learnable thing perfectly,[61] and if anyone claims a compound is more knowable, and an element is by

---

61 Even if the temporal order of learning is the same as the inherent order of knowability, the evidence here is complicated. Written letters are learned one at a time, but they are only known when they are associated with their sounds, most of which can be heard only as part of syllables (see note to 203B). And with tunes, perhaps singing differs from playing the harp, but a child who's been taught a tune might well sing it one or more octaves above what the teacher sang—that is, with none of the notes the same. Socrates is being deliberately playful, with serious intent.

its nature unknowable, we'll consider that, willingly or unwillingly, he's being playful.

Theae: Precisely so.

C   **Soc:** Well, still other demonstrations of this might make an appearance, as it seems to me, but let's not forget, on their account, to look at what was set in front of us, namely, whatever is meant by saying that when an articulation becomes present with a true opinion, the most complete knowledge comes about.

Theae: Then we ought to look.

Soc: Come then; what is "articulation" meant to signify to us? For it seems to me to mean any one of three things.

Theae: What are they?

D   **Soc:** The first would be making one's thinking apparent through sound with phrases and words, molding one's opinion into the stream flowing through the mouth as if into a mirror or water. Or doesn't such a thing seem to you to be an articulation?

Theae: It does to me. At any rate, we say that someone who does that is articulating.

Soc: Then again, everyone has the power to do this sooner or later, to indicate what seems so to him about each thing, who's not mute or disabled from the start; and so

E   all those who have any correct opinion obviously have it with an articulation, and correct opinion apart from knowledge won't come about any more anywhere.

Theae: True.

Soc: Well, let's not so easily condemn the person who declares knowledge to be what we're now examining for making no sense, since perhaps in saying it he didn't mean that, but that the one who's asked what each thing is should have the power to give the answer

207A   back to the questioner by means of its elements.

Theae: What, for example, do you mean, Socrates?

Soc: About a wagon, for example, Hesiod says "a hundred pieces of wood belong to a wagon,"[62] which I wouldn't have the power to state, nor, I suppose, would you, but we'd be quite satisfied, on being asked what a wagon is, if we had the capacity to say "wheels, axle, box, poles, crossbar."

Theae: Very much so.

Soc: But the questioner for his part might perhaps suppose, as he would if we had been asked for your name and had answered by its syllables, that we were ridiculous, *B* even though we have a correct opinion and articulated the things we articulated correctly, if we supposed that we were literate people and that we had and gave the articulation of the name Theaetetus in a literate way; he'd suppose there couldn't be any articulating of it knowledgeably until one had gotten all the way through each name by way of its letters along with a true opinion, as was surely stated in what went before.

Theae: That was stated.

Soc: Then that's the way he'd think about the wagon as well, that we have a correct opinion, but it's the one who has the power to go through the very being of it by way of *C* those hundred things, who by adding this has added an articulation to his true opinion, and instead of being capable of opinion has become artful and a knower about the very being of a wagon, having gone all the way through the whole by way of its elements.

Theae: Does he seem to you to be thinking well, Socrates?

Soc: If it seems that way to you, my companion, and you accept the going through by way of the elements as being the articulation about each thing, while going through it by compounds or by still larger things is inarticulate, tell me that in order that we may *D* examine it.

Theae: I accept it completely.

---

62 *Works and Days*, line 456, where the point is that someone might thoughtlessly assume it would be an easy thing to build a wagon.

Soc: Do you regard anyone whatever as a knower of anything whatever when the same thing sometimes seems to him to belong to one thing and sometimes to something else, or when he has the opinion that it's sometimes one thing and sometimes another that belongs to it?

Theae: By Zeus, not I.

Soc: Then are you forgetting that you yourself and everyone else did those very things in learning spelling at the beginning?

E

Theae: Do you mean sometimes considering that one letter but sometimes another belonged to the same syllable, and sometimes putting the same letter into the appropriate syllable but sometimes into a different one?

Soc: That's what I mean.

Theae: By Zeus, I haven't forgotten it, then, and I certainly don't consider people in that condition to have knowledge yet.

Soc: Then what? When, at such a time, someone writing "Theaetetus" supposes he needs to write theta and epsilon and writes it, and then again in trying to write "Theodorus" he supposes he needs to write tau and epsilon and writes it, will we claim he knows the first syllable of your names?

208A

Theae: But we just now agreed that someone who's in this condition doesn't yet know.

Soc: Then does anything prevent the same person from being in that condition about the second syllable as well, and the third, and the fourth?

Theae: Nothing at all.

Soc: Then at such a time, holding to the way through it by the letter, he'll write "Theaetetus" with a correct opinion, when he writes it in order?

Theae: That's clear.

Soc: And that's while still being without knowledge, but *B* having a correct opinion, as we're claiming?

Theae: Yes.

Soc: In fact it's while having an articulation along with a correct opinion, since he was writing it while holding to the way by the letter, which is just what we agreed an articulation is.[63]

Theae: True.

Soc: Therefore, my companion, there is correct opinion with an articulation, which one must not yet call knowledge.

Theae: It does run that risk.

Soc: So as it seems, our wealth was a dream when we supposed we had the truest articulation of knowledge. Or shall we not denounce it quite yet? For perhaps *C* someone will define it not as this, but as the form that's left out of the three, one of which we claimed would be set down as an articulation by the person who defines knowledge as correct opinion with an articulation.

Theae: You reminded me correctly, since there's still one left. For one was a sort of image of thinking in sound, and the other was the one just now mentioned as the road to the whole by way of the element; but what other third one do you mean?

Soc: Just the thing that most people would say: having some sign to say in what respect the thing in question differs from all things.

Theae: What articulation about what thing do you have as an example to tell me?

Soc: For example, if you want, about the sun, I suppose *D* it would be sufficient for you to accept that it is the brightest of the things going across the heavens around the earth.

Theae: Completely so.

---

63   In 207C, where the word for element is the same as the word here for letter.

Soc: Then grasp the reason for the sake of which it was stated, and it is the very thing we were saying just now, that as soon as you grasp the difference of each thing by which it differs from everything else, you'll grasp an articulation, as some people claim; but as long as you hang on to anything that's shared in common, your articulation will be about those things among which the commonness is shared.

E   **Theae:** I understand, and it seems to me to hold in a beautiful way to call such a thing an articulation.

Soc: Then whoever, along with a correct opinion about any of the beings whatever, gets hold in addition of its difference from everything else, will have become a knower of the very thing about which before he was someone with an opinion.

Theae: That's the way we're making the claim, anyway.

Soc: Now, though, Theaetetus, when we're up close what's been said has become like a sketch made of shadings, and I for one understand it absolutely not even a little bit; but as long as I was standing far back, it appeared to me to make some sense.

Theae: How in the world is that?

209A **Soc:** I'll show you, if I'll be able to. When I have a correct opinion about you, if I get hold in addition of your articulation, I'll recognize you, but if not, I'll have the opinion only.

Theae: Yes.

Soc: And an articulation was a putting into words of your differentness.

Theae: That's so.

Soc: So when I only had an opinion, I was touching on something else in my thinking, but not on any of those things by which you differ from everything else?

Theae: It seems not.

Soc: Therefore, I was thinking about something shared in common, which you have no more than does any other person.

Theae: Necessarily.   *B*

Soc: Come on, then, by Zeus. How in the world, in such a case, did I have an opinion about you any more than about anyone else whatever? For put it that I'm thinking that this is Theaetetus, whoever is a human being and has a nose and eyes and a mouth, and so on for each one of the parts of the body. Now is it possible that this sort of thinking will make me think of Theaetetus any more than of Theodorus, or of the least of the Mysians,[64] as the saying goes?

Theae: How could it?

Soc: But if I think of the one who has not only a nose and eyes, but also has the one squashed-in and the others   *C* popping out, it's again not anything about you I'll be thinking of, is it, any more than about myself or as many people as are of that sort?

Theae: Not at all.

Soc: But, I suppose, there will not have been an opinion about Theaetetus in me until this squashed-in-ness, as something different from the other squashed-in-nesses that I've seen, has deposited a memorial by imprinting it in me—and the same way with the other things you're made up of—which will recall you to me if I meet up with you tomorrow, and make me have correct opinions about you.

Theae: Most true.

Soc: Therefore, correct opinion too would be about the   *D* differentness of each thing.

Theae: It certainly appears so.

Soc: Then what more would it be to get hold in addition of an articulation with the correct opinion? For if it means having an additional opinion about the way in which

---

64   A people in Asia Minor considered contemptible; in *Gorgias* 521B, Callicles names them as somewhere below servile flatterers.

something differs from other things, it turns out to be a completely ridiculous requirement.

Theae: In what way?

Soc: It demands of us that, for things about which we have a correct opinion of the way they differ from other things, we get hold in addition of a correct opinion of the way they differ from other things. And so the twirling of a baton or a bat, or whatever the saying is, would mean nothing compared to this requirement, but it would more justly be called directions from a blind man; for to tell us to get hold in addition of those things that we have, in order that we might understand the things we have opinions about, seems to have a completely true-born resemblance to someone who's lost his sight.[65]

Theae: But tell me, what were you about to say just now that you got this out of?

Soc: If, my boy, to get hold of an articulation in addition tells us to recognize the differentness rather than to have an opinion about it, that would be a pleasant thing for the most beautiful articulation of the things that have to do with knowledge, since to recognize is presumably to take hold of knowledge, isn't it?

Theae: Yes.

Soc: Then as it seems, when it's asked what knowledge is, this account answers that it's a correct opinion along with a knowledge of differentness, since according to it, that would be the taking hold in addition of an articulation.

Theae: So it seems.

Soc: And it's totally silly, when we're inquiring about knowledge, to claim that it's correct opinion along with knowledge, whether about differentness or about anything whatever. Therefore, Theaetetus, neither

E

210A

---

65   The ironic resonance of the last clause is densely packed: the "knowledge" we have as a possession might necessarily be mere opinion, an active and attentive taking hold of it may be necessary for understanding it, a turning away from perception may be required, and that whole process might be the way knowledge is truly born out of ourselves.

perception nor true opinion, nor even an articulation   *B*
that's become attached to a true opinion would be
knowledge.

Theae: It seems not.

Soc: Then are we still pregnant and in labor with anything
about knowledge, dear fellow, or have we given birth
to everything?

Theae: Yes we have, by Zeus, and I at least have said more,
on account of you, than what I used to have in myself.

Soc: Then our art of midwifery declares that all these
things came into being as wind-eggs and aren't worth
rearing?

Theae: Absolutely.

Soc: Then if you try to become pregnant with other things
after these, Theaetetus, and you do come to be so,   *C*
you'll be full of better things on account of the present
examination, and if you're barren, you'll be less severe
with those who are around you and gentler,[66] being
moderate and not supposing that you know things
you don't know. For that and nothing more is the
only sort of thing my art has the power to do, and I
don't know any of the things all the others do who
are and have been great and wondrous men, but I and
my mother have been allotted this midwifery as our
portion from a god, she among women and I among   *D*
the young and well-born, all those, that is, that are
beautiful. But now there's something I need to go and
face in the courtyard of the king-archon, in response to
the indictment which Meletus has drawn up against
me; but at dawn, Theodorus, let's meet here again.[67]

---

66   Theaetetus doesn't seem to be inclined to these faults, but Socrates could be
concerned to save him from the discomfort Theodorus reveals in his repeated
irritable complaints throughout the dialogue about most students, most
philosophers, and most people in general. (See 144A-B, 179E-180C, 170D-E.)

67   The indictment is the one that resulted in Socrates's trial and death; the dialogue
is thus framed between allusions involving the deaths of Theaetetus and
Socrates. The appointment for the next day is kept, and results in one long
conversation that spans the *Sophist* and the *Statesman*.